THE KINGFISHER FACTS AND RECORDS BOOK OF SPACE

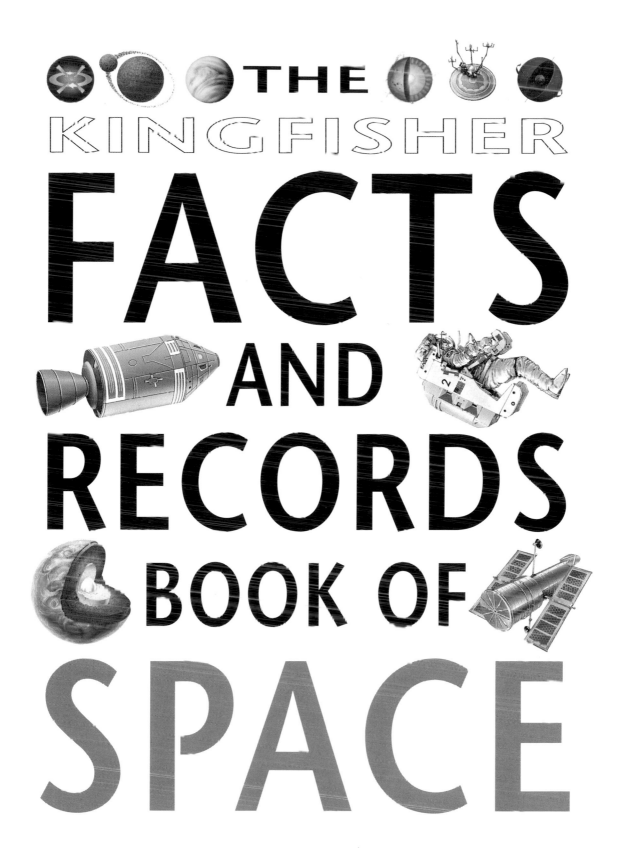

THE KINGFISHER FACTS AND RECORDS BOOK OF SPACE

KING*fisher*

NEW YORK

Author	Clive Gifford
Deputy Art Director	Mike Buckley
Art Editor	Keith Davis
Designer	Joe Conneally
Editors	Fergus Collins, Clive Wilson
Picture Researcher	Tara McCormack
DTP Coordinator	Nicky Studdart
Production Controller	Jacquie Horner, Caroline Hansell
Artwork Archivists	Wendy Allison, Steve Robinson
Indexer	Sue Lightfoot

KINGFISHER
Larousse Kingfisher Chambers Inc.
80 Maiden Lane
New York, New York 10038
www.lkcpub.com

Produced by Scintilla Editorial
33 Great Portland Street
London W1W 8QG

First published in 2001
1 3 5 7 9 10 8 6 4 2

1TR/0201/TWP/MAR/SMA150

LIBRARY OF CONGRESS CATOLOGING-IN-PUBLICATION DATA
has been applied for.

ISBN 0-7534-5363-0

Printed in Singapore

CONTENTS

SOLAR SYSTEM

SUN AND STARS

UNIVERSE

SKYWATCHING

PEOPLE AND SPACE

THE FUTURE

SOLAR SYSTEM

The solar system is made up of nine planets, over 60 moons, and millions of asteroids and comets. At its center is the largest object in the system, the sun. It is the sun's huge gravitational pull that holds the solar system together and controls the movement of the planets.

Birth of a Star System

Astronomers believe the sun formed around five billion years ago from a huge cloud of gas and dust called the solar nebula. As the solar nebula began to shrink, it pulled in more and more gas and dust into its center, became hotter, and started to form a central orb, surrounded by a spinning disk of gas and dust. Nuclear processes (see page 24) started within the central orb, and the orb became the sun we rely on today for heat and light. Eventually, the remaining material in the disk came together to form the planets and their natural satellites, or moons.

Between Mars and Jupiter are a large number of rocks called asteroids. These form the asteroid belt.

BORN FROM DUST
In (1), the solar system is a spinning cloud of dust. Gravity within the cloud pulls matter toward the center (2), where nuclear reactions create the embryonic sun. The rest of the dust spins around the central sun (3), coming together to form nine orbiting planets (4).

A spherical region of comets called the Oort Cloud surrounds the solar system.

MERCURY   VENUS   EARTH   MARS   JUPITER

Mercury 0.39 AU
Venus 0.72 AU
Earth 1 AU
Mars 1.52 AU
Asteroid belt
Jupiter 5.20 AU
Saturn 9.54 AU
Uranus 19.2 AU

1 2 3 4 5 6 7 8 9 10 11 12 13 14 15 16 17 18 19 20 21 22 23 24

FACTS AND FIGURES

The inner six planets were known to people of ancient times. The outer three were discovered using telescopes.

Only Jupiter and Neptune have a greater gravitational pull at their surfaces than Earth.

It takes sunlight 3 minutes, 13 seconds to reach Mercury, but 5 hours, 28 minutes, and 19 seconds to reach Pluto.

The Oort Cloud, named after Jan Oort, who first suggested its existence in the 1950s, is 1.6 light-years across.

Planetary Motion

Each planet turns on its axis. The time it takes to complete a 360° turn is called a planet's rotational period, or day. It takes Earth just over 23 hours, 56 minutes to complete a rotation. Planets travel around the sun on a path called an orbit. The time taken to complete one orbit is an orbital period, or year. Each planet has a different orbital period. The farther it is from the sun, the longer the orbit. For centuries, orbits were thought to be circular. We now know that all planets travel in oval, or elliptical, orbits—sometimes closer to the sun than at other times. The point at which a planet is farthest from the sun is called aphelion. When it is closest to the sun, it is said to be at perihelion.

In 1995, a planet was discovered—for the first time—in another star system. It is 150 times bigger than Earth.

Measuring Distances

Astronomers use a special unit of measurement to represent the huge distances involved in the solar system and universe. The distance between stars is measured in light-years. Light travels about 185,000 miles every second. In a light-year, it journeys around 6 trillion miles. Within the solar system, the basic unit of distance is the astronomical unit (AU). This is the average distance between Earth and the sun—92,800,000 miles. Neptune, for example, is 30 AUs away from the sun—that is, 30 times farther from the sun than Earth.

Of the planets, Venus has the most circular orbit and Pluto the most elliptical.

DATABANK

INPUT

Q How big is the solar system?

Q Is our star system the only place in the universe that has planets?

Q What's the difference between a planet and a moon?

OUTPUT

A The solar system fills an area approximately 9 trillion miles in diameter.

A Astronomers have recently discovered as many as 50 planets in other solar systems.

A A planet is a body that orbits a star. A moon, or natural satellite, is an object that orbits a planet.

SATURN   URANUS   NEPTUNE   PLUTO

PLANETARY POSITIONS
Reading from left to right, this chart shows the relative distances of the planets from the sun in astronomical units (AU).

Pluto 29.6 AU at its closest   Neptune 30.1 AU   Pluto 49.50 AU at its farthest

26 27 28 29 30 31 32 33 34 35 36 37 38 39 40 41 42 43 44 45 46 47 48 49 50

EARTH AND ITS MOON

The third planet from the sun, Earth is the only place where life is known to exist. This is partly because it is the right distance from the sun, preventing Earth's water from being boiled away or becoming permanently frozen.

Atmosphere: extends 310 mi. into space

Mantle: 1,860 mi. thick

Outer core: 1,360 mi. thick

Inner Core: 1,550 mi. in diameter

Crust: 5–22 mi. thick

Earth's Structure

The fifth largest planet in the solar system, Earth is larger than the three other rocky inner planets—Mercury, Venus, and Mars. Beneath its solid crust lies a hot, rocky layer known as the mantle. This is solid, but can move like ice in a glacier. The crust is formed from 15 plates, which float on the mantle. Beneath the mantle lies the outer core. Made of molten iron, this generates Earth's powerful magnetic field. The inner core is solid iron.

FIERY FURNACE
The temperature at Earth's core may reach 13,000°F. Heat rises through the mantle in convection currents.

Earth's surface area is 316 million sq. mi. The moon's surface area is about 24 million sq. mi.

HOT BEGINNINGS
Earth formed five billion years ago from matter left over from the sun's creation. Initially hot, it cooled and shrank over time.

As Earth cooled and condensed, it became the densest planet in the entire solar system.

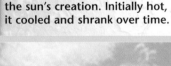 Harboring Life

From space, Earth's blue color, white polar caps, and wispy atmosphere mark the planet out as something special. With its moderate temperature range and average surface temperature of 59°F, Earth allows liquid water to exist in huge quantities on its surface. Water is essential to life, as is oxygen, a gas. Earth's atmosphere, which rises more than 61 miles from its surface, is made up of 21 percent oxygen, 77 percent nitrogen, and small amounts of argon, water vapor, carbon dioxide, and other gases.

FACTS AND FIGURES

Earth's diameter at the equator is 7, 900 mi. Its circumference at the equator is 24,902 mi.

The moon is a cold place with an average temperature of -4°F. The temperature can drop as low as -243°F.

The largest crater on the moon is called Hertzsprung and has a diameter of 366 mi.

If Earth's ice melted, the sea levels would rise by 330 ft. Today only 30 percent of Earth's surface is land.

Earth is on average about 93 million miles from the sun, and the moon is 238,857 miles from Earth.

Earth's four main oceans, the Atlantic, Pacific, Indian, and Arctic, hold 97.2 percent of Earth's water.

LIVING PLANET
Seen from the moon, Earth's atmosphere seems very thin and fragile. Astronauts report being greatly moved by the sight.

Lunar Surface

A rocky, pitted place, the moon is a quarter of the size of Earth. Large lava plains, called maria, form most of the side of the moon we can see. Of its 1,940 named features, 1,545 are craters created mainly by asteroids crashing into its surface. The moon has no atmosphere, winds, or flowing water to erode its surface. What we see there has remained unchanged for three or four billion years.

With no atmosphere to carry sound vibrations, the moon is a completely silent place.

Sea of Showers

Sea of Serenity

Apollo 15

Apollo 17

Sea of Crises

Ocean of Storms

Sea of Tranquillity

Sea of Clouds

Apollo 11

Sea of Fertility

Apollo 12

Apollo 14

Apollo 16

Sea of Nectar

Sea of Moisture

NEAR SIDE OF THE MOON

MOON FORMATION
The moon may have formed from debris expelled into orbit around Earth by a collision between Earth and a huge object.

Phases of the Moon

In its orbit around Earth, the moon always shows the same side to us. The far side is often called the dark side because it cannot be viewed from Earth. The way the sun's light hits the surface of the moon makes it appear to change shape within its monthly orbit. These different shapes are called phases, and there are five main types: new, crescent, quarter, gibbous, and full. When the moon is new and dark to us, the far side is lit by sunshine. We think of Earth's gravity keeping the moon in orbit around our planet, but the moon pulls back, too. It's the moon's pull that creates the sea and ocean tides.

HORIZON
Because the moon is so much smaller than Earth, horizons appear closer to the observer than they do on Earth.

MOONSHINE
At new moon, the unlit side of the moon faces Earth, so it seems invisible. At full moon we see the whole sunlit face.

Sunlight

Last quarter

Waning gibbous

Waning crescent

Full moon

New moon

Waxing crescent

Earth

Waxing gibbous

First quarter

Sunlight

MERCURY AND VENUS

Mercury and Venus are the two planets closest to the sun. They both are made of solid rock, they are warmer than Earth, and they do not have moons. Yet probes have shown they are very different from each other.

Caloris Basin

Mapping Mercury

Caught up in the sun's glare, Mercury is hard to examine from Earth. Most of what we know about the planet comes from the *Mariner 10* mission of 1974–75. The probe's thousands of photographs showed a dead world, full of craters and solidified lava flows. The craters are believed to have been created more than four billion years ago when debris left over from the formation of the solar system crashed into the planet.

Mercury has a wrinkled surface. This may be because its cooling iron core caused the planet to shrink.

HOLE PUNCH
The Caloris Basin is a 1,806 mi.-wide crater made when an object at least 62 mi. in diameter collided with Mercury.

Temperature Extremes

The sun's strong gravitational pull has slowed Mercury's rotation so much that the planet's day lasts 176 Earth days. This, along with the almost nonexistent atmosphere, gives the planet's surface time to become fiercely hot when facing the sun. It also allows the surface to cool to well below freezing when it is in shadow. The temperature extremes on Mercury have been measured at -280°F at its coldest and 800°F at its hottest.

MARINER 10
Mariner 10 discovered that Mercury has a weak magnetic field produced by the planet's large core.

BIG SUN
When viewed from the surface of Mercury, the sun appears 6.3 times brighter than it does from Earth.

DATABANK

Q Has a probe ever landed on Mercury? If not, how close has one flown to the surface?

A The *Mariner 10* probe flew as close as 470 mi. from Mercury's surface during its 1975 mission.

Q Have any probes actually landed on the surface of Venus?

A Four Russian Venera probes have landed and sent back photographs and data.

Earth's Twin?

Venus is known as the morning or evening star because it appears just after sunset or just before sunrise.

Named after the Roman goddess of beauty, Venus is the brightest planet visible from Earth. Separated from Earth by just 26 million miles and almost the same size, Venus is sometimes referred to as Earth's twin. Such a name can be deceiving because Venus is a desolate rocky planet, hostile to life. With a surface temperature of around 896°F, the planet is hotter than Mercury —despite being farther from the sun. Its surface has many craters— largely the result of volcanic activity.

SIZE COMPARISON
Venus is 7,500 mi. wide, while Mercury has a diameter of just 3,024 mi. By comparison our moon's diameter is 2,155 mi.

Most sunlight reflected by cloud layer

Little heat escapes

Upper cloud layer

Middle cloud layer

Lower cloud layer

A little sunlight gets through.

Heat reflected from the ground is trapped.

SMOG WORLD
The thick layer of carbon dioxide cloud acts like a blanket, stopping most of the sun's heat from getting away.

Heavy Atmosphere

Venus is cloaked in a thick, choking blanket of carbon dioxide. Only about 20 percent of the sunlight that strikes Venus reaches the ground, yet the planet has an incredibly high surface temperature. This is the result of the heavy atmosphere trapping heat on the planet's surface, causing what is called the greenhouse effect. The atmosphere also presses down hard on the planet's surface. The pressure is similar to being under water on earth at a depth of 3,000 feet. Large clouds within the atmosphere rain sulfuric acid onto the planet's surface. If we could land on Venus, scientists believe that the sky would appear a gloomy orange color.

FIRE AND BRIMSTONE
Volcanic reactions on Venus have sent huge amounts of sulfur into the atmosphere. These form acidic clouds.

RADAR MAP
Because Venus' atmosphere is so thick, radar must be used to build a picture of its features, such as the mountain Maat Mons.

MARS

Named after the Roman god of war, Mars is the only planet whose surface is visible—with the aid of a telescope—from Earth. It is also the least hostile planet and may even once have supported life.

The Red Planet

The fourth planet from the sun, Mars is about half the size of Earth with a diameter of just 4,208 miles. It is approximately one and a half times farther from the sun than Earth. Its orbit around the sun is oval-shaped, or elliptical, and its distance from the sun varies by up to 25 million miles. Half of its surface shows signs of past volcanic activity, with many volcanoes and what may have been lava-flow channels scouring its rocky, desertlike surface. Mars remains tilted on its axis in a similar way to Earth as it orbits the sun. This gives it similar seasons to those on Earth, although martian seasons are almost twice as long.

SCARRED PLANET
At 2,480 mi. long and reaching 3 to 6 mi. deep, the Valles Marineris is the largest canyon system in the solar system.

OLYMPUS MONS
About 372 mi. in diameter and with a crater 56 mi. wide, Mars' giant volcano is the largest in the solar system.

DATABANK

INPUT	OUTPUT
Q Are there really irrigation channels on Mars?	**A** No. The channels were possibly made by ancient rivers.
Q Does Mars have an atmosphere like Earth's?	**A** No. It is 95 percent carbon dioxide and 0.03 percent oxygen.
Q Why is Mars the red planet? Is the planet going rusty?	**A** Yes! Iron in the soil reacts with oxygen, creating iron oxide.
Q When did the first mission to Mars take place?	**A** In 1962, the Soviet Union sent the *Mars 1* probe.

Moons of Mars

Mars has two irregular-shaped moons, Phobos and Deimos. Once they might have been asteroids that were caught in the planet's gravity. Both moons were discovered by astronomer Asaph Hall in August 1877. He named them after the sons of the god of war in Greek mythology. Phobos orbits Mars in only seven and a half hours. Its month is a third of the length of a martian day.

Phobos

Deimos

Life on Mars?

About 4 billion years ago, Mars may have been warm enough for rivers and oceans to flow over its surface.

From ancient times until the 21st century, people have thought that life might exist on Mars. Early astronomers believed the darker areas of Mars' surface were vegetation. In Victorian times, some notable astronomers claimed to see straight lines etched on the planet's surface, which they believed were irrigation channels. Data collected by orbiting probes and landers reveals a more realistic picture. Mars does not appear to contain any form of life. Its thin atmosphere, with only 1 percent of the atmospheric pressure of Earth, has almost no water, does little to raise the average temperature from well below freezing, and does not shield the surface from lethal doses of ultraviolet rays. Debate does continue, however, about whether or not Mars supported life millions of years ago.

Future crewless missions to Mars may try to grow bacteria or manufacture fuel on the planet.

FACTS AND FIGURES

The closest Mars gets to the sun is 128 million mi. The nearest it passes to Earth is about 35 million mi. away.

A martian day, known as a sol, lasts 24 hours, 37 minutes, while a year lasts 687 Earth days.

Mars' surface temperature averages -81°F but varies from an icy -198°F to a pleasant 80°F.

In 1971, *Mariner 9* orbited Mars successfully and took 7,329 photographs of the planet's surface

Phobos orbits Mars at an average distance of just 5,709 mi. Its largest crater, Stickney, is 6 mi. across.

Deimos is so small and its gravity so weak that a speed of only 22 mph is needed to escape its gravity.

Just 9 mi. long, Deimos orbits at over 14,260 mi. from Mars. It is the second smallest moon in the solar system.

At times, Mars appears as the third brightest object in the night sky, after Venus and the moon.

SURVEYOR
Global Surveyor reached Mars in 1997 and orbited as close as 217 mi. from the surface during its 18-month-long mission. It mapped the planet and its weather in incredible detail.

WATER PROBE
Scientists have built probes to test below Mars' surface. The Russian *Mars 96* mission carried the *Penetrator* (above), which had a 20-foot-long probe. Sadly, the *Mars 96* craft exploded on the launchpad.

GENTLER PLANET
Despite lacking water and a breathable atmosphere, Mars' environment is not as hostile as other rocky planets', like Venus.

JUPITER

The giant of our solar system, Jupiter is the fifth planet from the sun and is 1,300 times bigger than Earth. Its mass is more than two and a half times the total of all the other planets combined.

- Metallic liquid hydrogen
- Liquid hydrogen
- Iron core
- Outer atmosphere
- Red spot

Jupiter's Structure

Jupiter is a gas giant with a gravity 2.7 times stronger than Earth's. Around 90 percent of the planet is made of hydrogen, with helium making up almost all of the remainder. Jupiter's outer layers are hydrogen and helium gas. Below this, tremendous pressure forces the two gases to act like a liquid metal. Here, powerful magnetic fields are generated, strong enough to send out radio waves that can be picked up on earth. The planet's core is thought to be compressed rock and iron. Scientists have discovered that Jupiter is shrinking. This process helps to generate the extreme temperatures found at the core, which astronomers estimate to be as high as 54,000°F.

Jupiter has a thin ring circling it. Although not as impressive as Saturn's rings, it is 19 mi. thick and 4,030 mi. wide.

ME AND MY SHADOW
Taken by the Hubble Space Telescope, this photograph shows the moon Io—and its shadow—orbiting Jupiter.

Moons of Jupiter

So far, sixteen moons have been located around Jupiter. The four largest, Io, Europa, Ganymede, and Callisto, are known together as the Galilean moons after the Italian astronomer Galileo. He was the first to examine them with a telescope, in 1610. Ganymede is the solar system's largest moon. At 3,266 miles in diameter, it is larger than the planets Mercury and Pluto. Io has the most volcanic activity in the solar system. Its volcanoes send plumes of gas up to 155 miles high. The smallest of Jupiter's moons is Leda. With a diameter of only 5 miles across, it is the smallest moon in our solar system.

EASILY SPOTTED
Jupiter's four largest moons, Io, Ganymede, Europa, and Callisto, can be seen from Earth by using a telescope.

Europa

Callisto

Ganymede

Io

HOT WHEN PULLED
The gravities of Jupiter, Ganymede, and Europa play tug-of-war with Io, heating the moon and making its interior molten.

DATABANK

INPUT	OUTPUT
Q Who first measured Jupiter, and when did this occur?	**A** British astronomer James Bradley first measured it in 1733.
Q When did scientists find out that Jupiter had rings like Saturn?	**A** In 1979, the *Voyager 1* probe made a flyby of the giant planet.
Q Why are scientists so interested in Jupiter's moon, Europa?	**A** There is a chance that life could exist under Europa's icy surface.
Q How big is Jupiter in comparison to the sun?	**A** Jupiter is just one thousandth of the sun's mass.

Fast Spinner

For such a huge planet, Jupiter spins incredibly fast, completing its day in under ten hours. At the equator, the speed of rotation is 26,061 mph—more than 25 times as fast as Earth. The huge forces created by this speed make Jupiter bulge out an extra 5,580 miles at its equator. Jupiter's turning speed and the heat rising from the planet's core—which is hotter than the sun's surface—generate its unusual weather patterns. Violent storms whip across much of its surface, stretching clouds out into bands parallel with the equator. Where the different bands of cloud meet, extremely violent storm systems develop. Some of the largest are visible with a telescope from Earth, such as the Great Red Spot.

In 1994, fragments of the comet Shoemaker-Levy 9 (S-L 9) smashed into Jupiter, leaving huge, dark marks.

GUSTY GIANT
The *Galileo* orbiter dropped a probe into Jupiter's gassy atmosphere in 1995. This probe measured the winds blowing through the atmosphere at a ferocious but fairly constant 329 mph.

FACTS AND FIGURES

Jupiter's average distance from the sun is 463 million mi. It takes 11 years, 315 days to make one orbit.

NASA's *Galileo* probe reached Jupiter in 1995. It orbited the planet 10 times over 22 months.

Jupiter's magnetic field is 20,000 times stronger than Earth's, and may stretch 1 million mi. from the planet.

The moon Callisto is covered with craters. It consists of 60 percent rock and iron and 40 percent ice and water.

Sinope orbits Jupiter at a distance of 14.7 million mi. —the largest orbit of any of the solar system's moons.

The color of the Great Red Spot may be the result of compounds of phosphorus or sulfur.

NASTY SPOT
Jupiter's Great Red Spot is an enormous hurricane that has raged for the last 300 years. Two to three times the diameter of Earth, the spot rotates counterclockwise once every six days. Winds blow throughout this huge area at speeds of around 280 mph.

SATURN

The ringed planet is the sixth from the sun, and the second largest after Jupiter. It is the flattest planet in the solar system because of the incredibly high speed at which it rotates.

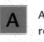

Saturn has such a low density that if it were possible to immerse it in water, it would float.

 ## A Rock and Gas Giant

The composition of Saturn has long been something of a mystery. Once thought to be formed entirely of gas, this giant planet is now believed to have a rocky core at its center. This core, estimated at between 12,400 and 18,600 miles across, is surrounded by a shell of metallic liquid hydrogen that helps generate Saturn's magnetic field. Liquid hydrogen extends out from the center for thousands of miles. This is surrounded by Saturn's atmosphere, which is made up mainly of hydrogen and helium.

FACTS AND FIGURES

Saturn takes 29.46 Earth years to orbit the sun—at an average distance of nearly 1 billion miles.

At its equator, Saturn's diameter is 74,700 miles, while at its poles the diameter is 67,700 miles.

Saturn has circulating bands of clouds. The planet's fastest winds race at up to 1,100 mph.

On Saturn the sun appears 1 percent as bright as it does on Earth. The average temperature is an icy –184°F.

Pan is Saturn's smallest moon. At just 12 miles in diameter, it is smaller than many asteroids.

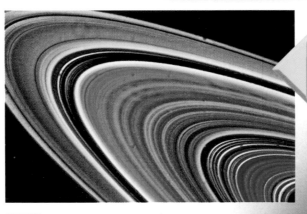

COMET TALE
Saturn's rings may have formed from a comet that strayed into the planet's gravitational field.

 ## The Rings

Galileo first observed something strange about Saturn in 1610, but his telescope was so weak he thought Saturn was a triple planet. Then in 1655, Christian Huygens confirmed the existence of the now familiar rings. Scientists have since identified over 10,000 separate rings, each made up of millions of tiny particles of rock and ice, arranged in bands of different densities.

DISAPPEARING
Every 14 or 15 years, Saturn's rings turn edge-on to Earth, and disappear. With the glare from the rings gone, it becomes easier to see Saturn's other features. Thirteen of Saturn's moons were discovered during such times.

Although over 155,000 miles in diameter, Saturn's rings are no more than 19 miles thick.

THICK ATMOSPHERE
Probes found three layers in Saturn's atmosphere—ammonia, ammonium sulfide, and water-bearing clouds.

VOYAGER 1 & 2
Much of what we know about Saturn has come from the space probes *Voyager 1* and *2*, which were launched in 1977.

Many Moons

As recently as 30 years ago, Saturn was thought to have just 10 moons. Today 23 satellites have been identified—but there are probably more. Some are only chunks of rock just a few miles across, orbiting the planet close to the rings. Others, like Dione, are over 600 miles across and circle Saturn at a distance of several million miles. Most remarkable is Titan, which at 3,200 miles in diameter is bigger than the planet Mercury.

Titan intrigues astronomers because it has a nitrogen-based atmosphere—just like Earth's.

MODERN-DAY EXPLORER
The *Cassini* orbiter will reach Saturn in 2004. It will drop the *Huygens* probe to explore Titan's atmosphere and surface.

THE OUTER PLANETS

Lying many millions of miles away, Uranus, Neptune, and Pluto were unknown until powerful telescopes were developed. Over the last 25 years, probes have given us further tantalizing glimpses of these distant worlds.

ON EDGE
Uranus appears to lie on its side so that one pole—and then the other—faces the sun on the planet's long orbit.

 ## Uranus

Uranus orbits the sun from an average distance of 1,780 million miles away. Its interior is believed to consist of a tiny rocky core, surrounded by clouds of methane ice. The planet's outer layers are composed of hydrogen and helium gas. Uranus has 15 moons, the largest is 90 miles in diameter and the smallest just 16 miles across. All are named after English literary characters. Some of Uranus' rings were first noticed in 1977. Nearly a decade later, *Voyager 2* detected a total of 11 rings made of very dark rocks, ice crystals, and dust.

Twice as far away from us as Saturn, Uranus is a tiny green disk when viewed through a telescope.

 ## *Voyager 2*

Our knowledge of Uranus and Neptune was limited until the *Voyager 2* mission. Launched in 1977, *Voyager 2* journeyed past Jupiter in 1979, Saturn in 1981, Uranus in 1986, and Neptune in 1989. *Voyager 2* made a number of discoveries, including six of Neptune's moons and nine moons around Uranus—all new to astronomers. The probe also mapped details of the planets, including Neptune's fierce winds and Uranus' rings.

EXPLORER
Voyager 2 used nuclear power instead of solar panels to provide fuel. The craft featured 16 small rocket thrusters, which were used to correct its course as it journeyed to the far reaches of the solar system.

FACTS AND FIGURES

Uranus was first discovered by the astronomer William Herschel in 1781. At first he thought it might be a comet.

Uranus is 31,620 mi. in diameter. Its day is 17 hours, 14 minutes long. Its year equals 84 Earth years.

Neptune is 36,690 mi. in diameter. Its day is 16 hours, 7 minutes long, while a year is 165 Earth years.

Johann Galle discovered the planet Neptune in 1846 when it was noticed that its gravity affected Uranus' orbit.

William Herschel originally wanted to name Uranus after the English king, George III, but he was overruled.

Pluto's diameter is 1,395 mi. Its day lasts 6 Earth days, 9 hours. Its year equals 248 Earth years.

The average temperature on Pluto is roughly about -382°F although this varies during the planet's orbit.

TRITON
Neptune's biggest moon, Triton, is the solar system's coldest land surface, with a temperature of -391°F.

CHURNING SPOT
The Great Dark Spot in Neptune's hydrogen, helium, and methane atmosphere is large enough to swallow Earth.

 # Neptune

Neptune orbits the sun from an average of 2,788 million miles away. The temperature of its atmosphere is estimated to be -346°F. Like Uranus it has rings, although Neptune's five (or more) rings are more faint. Neptune has eight moons, the largest of which, Triton, is extraordinary. It is 1,286 miles across and has a crust made of rock-hard ice. Plumes of nitrogen gas erupt from its surface, like geysers. Triton orbits in the opposite direction to the way Neptune rotates.

Neptune appears blue from space because it has methane ice crystals in its atmosphere.

 # Pluto

The American astronomer Clyde Tombaugh discovered Pluto in 1930. About a tenth of the size of Earth, Pluto is relatively unknown because no telescope has seen it clearly.

We do know that Pluto has one moon, called Charon, which is half the size of the planet it orbits. Pluto has an eccentric orbit that carries it as close as 2,774 million miles from the sun and as far from it as 4,573 million miles. This means that for 20 out of every 250 years, Pluto moves inside Neptune's orbit, and Neptune becomes the outermost planet.

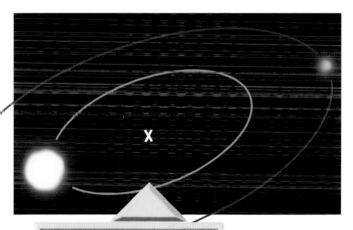

SPACE WALTZ
Pluto and its moon Charon orbit each other around a center of gravity (X). They always show each other the same face.

ROCKY OUTPOST
Pluto may have a rocky core surrounded by layers of ice and frozen methane. It could once have been a moon of Neptune.

PLUTO AND CHARON
If you were to stand on the surface of Pluto, the moon Charon would seem very large—seven times the size of our moon.

COMETS AND OTHER BODIES

Planets, moons, and the sun are not the only bodies in the solar system. Asteroids form a large belt between Mars and Jupiter. Comets orbit the sun from great distances and sometimes can even be seen from Earth. Meteors and meteorites are rocks that enter Earth's atmosphere.

Asteroids

Asteroids are chunks of rock, metal, or a combination of the two that orbit the sun. Over 90 percent of all the solar system's asteroids lie in the 213-million-mile-wide asteroid belt that is found between Mars and Jupiter. This doughnut-shaped body of objects is believed to be the remains of a planet that never properly formed when the solar system was in its infancy. Larger asteroids are sometimes referred to as the minor planets. Ceres, the first asteroid to be discovered, is also the largest, with a diameter of about 620 miles. Yet Vesta, the third largest asteroid, is the only member of the belt close enough and large enough to be seen with the naked eye.

Over 200,000 tons of space rock enters Earth's atmosphere every year, and over 3,000 meteorites land.

SPACE ROCKS
The asteroid Ida (left) is one of thousands of large objects (above) that make up the asteroid belt. Ida orbits the sun just like a tiny planet, and even has its own miniature moon called Dactyl.

Meteors and Meteorites

Meteors are small pieces of rock and dust that enter Earth's atmosphere. Most are fragments of asteroids, but some are small pieces of debris from Mars, the moon, or comets. Most meteors burn up in the atmosphere, forming streaks of light, called shooting stars, in the night sky. Some larger chunks of debris do not burn up completely and hit Earth's surface. These are called meteorites. Most meteorites are made of rock, although some are made of iron or a mixture of rock and iron. All are eagerly sought by collectors.

SURVIVAL OF THE BIGGEST
The vast majority of meteors burn up about 31 mi. above the ground. Large ones occasionally make it through to strike Earth.

DATABANK

Q Do we have evidence that anyone has been killed by a meteorite?

A No humans. A dog in Nakhla, Egypt, was killed by a meteorite in 1911.

Q When will Halley's Comet next be seen?

A It passed closest to Earth in the 1980s and will be back in the 2050s.

BOLT FROM THE BLUE
Many people believe that a meteorite impact changed Earth's climate and wiped out the dinosaurs 65 million years ago.

STREAKER
When you look at a comet in the night sky, it does not appear to be moving fast, but it may be traveling over 99,200 mph.

CLOSE-UP
Jets of gas escape from the surface of the nucleus of a comet and are blown by the solar wind to form a tail.

 # Comets

Comets are like huge, dirty snowballs that orbit the sun. The head of a comet contains a nucleus just a few miles across and made up of rocky dust bound in ice. As a comet gets closer to the sun, some of the ice melts, releasing dust. This forms a glowing head, called a coma, and a tail. The time it takes a comet to orbit around the sun is called its period. Some comets have short periods, others have long periods. A short period comet has an orbit that takes less than 200 years. A comet is usually named after the person who discovers it. The most famous was discovered in 1682 by astronomer Edmund Halley. He predicted the comet's return every 76 years.

In 1983, the comet IRAS-Araki-Alcock passed within 3 million mi. of Earth—one of the closest on record.

FACTS AND FIGURES

Although many orbit close to Earth, asteroids are thought to strike Earth only once every 250,000 years.

The biggest meteorite found on Earth—in Namibia, Africa—measured 9 ft. by 8 ft. and weighed 60 tons.

The largest known comet was the Comet Flaugergues of 1811. Its coma was estimated to be 1,116,000 mi. wide.

The Great Comet of 1843 possessed a tail long enough to wrap around the Earth's equator 8,000 times.

An estimated 10 trillion comets lie at the edge of the solar system, making up what is called the Oort Cloud.

Comets are less dense than water or air. If all the comets were combined, they would weigh little more than Earth.

Comet Encke takes just three years to orbit the sun, while other comets may take thousands of years.

BACK AGAIN
Halley's Comet is recorded many times in history, such as when it appeared over Jerusalem in A.D. 66 (far left). Halley noticed a pattern in the records, from which he predicted when the comet would appear again.

STARS AND STAR TYPES

On a clear night, you can see over 2,500 faint pinpricks of light dotted across the night sky—just a fraction of the billions of stars that exist in the universe. Stars come in many sizes and burn with a surprising variety of brightnesses.

Measuring Brightness

How bright a star appears from Earth—its apparent magnitude—is not a guide to how brightly it shines throughout the universe. Astronomers use a scale called absolute magnitude, which is a measure of a star's brightness if viewed from a distance of 32.6 light-years. The smaller the magnitude number, the brighter the star. The dimmest stars observed so far have absolute magnitudes of over 18, while the brightest stars have magnitudes of -8 or less. Each whole-number step on the magnitude scale equals an increase or decrease in brightness of 2.5 times. This means that a star of the first magnitude is 100 times brighter than a star of the sixth magnitude—the faintest stars visible to the naked eye.

TWINKLE, TWINKLE, LITTLE STAR
A star may appear to twinkle because air movement in Earth's atmosphere makes the light from the star twist and bend.

LITTLE AND LARGE
Betelgeuse (right) is a giant, but tiny G1623b (with its larger companion below) is just a tenth of the mass of our sun.

The *Hipparcos* probe, launched in 1989 by the European Space Agency, measures star positions accurately.

Binary Stars

Many stars do not exist alone like our sun. Instead they belong to a star system, which contains two or more stars. Binary star systems with two stars account for about one fifth of all stars observed so far. In some binary star systems, the two may be extremely close, orbiting each other in a few hours. In other systems, the stars may be many millions of miles apart. Binary stars interest astronomers because by measuring the effect of each star's gravity on the other, it is possible to calculate each one's mass.

FACTS AND FIGURES

The use of magnitude for measuring a star's brightness was devised in 130 B.C. by Hipparchus of Nicaea.

A star with an apparent magnitude of 9 is the faintest star observable from Earth using binoculars.

The smallest star observed so far is called UV Ceti B. It has a mass of only 3.5 percent of the sun.

The brightest object in the night sky (except the moon) is the planet Venus, with an apparent magnitude of -4.

If Betelgeuse replaced our sun in the solar system, its outer atmosphere would extend past Jupiter.

NEIGHBORS
Although binary stars appear to revolve around each other, they are really orbiting a common center of gravity (X).

The measures of a star's brightness shown here are absolute magnitudes.

CAPELLA
About 1,200 light-years away, this type G appears as the sixth brightest star. Its magnitude is 0.4.

BETELGEUSE
This type M star is 310 light-years away and has a magnitude of −7.2. Its size makes it seem even brighter.

OUR SUN
Our own local star is a type G star, which means that it is not particularly hot—in relation to other stars.

Temperature and Color

Stars are classified in many ways, from their size and position to their color. A star's color usually depends on its temperature. The hottest stars glow blue-white, and the coolest stars are an orange-red color. Astronomers divide nearly all stars up into seven classes of what they call "spectral classes," depending on their temperature. These run from type O, the hottest, through types B, A, F, G, K, to type M, the coolest. The sun is a type G star.

While most stars are too far away to see in detail, scientists have found a bright patch on Betelgeuse's surface.

VEGA
Just 25 light-years away, Vega is a type A star, one of the brightest stars we can see. Its magnitude is 0.6.

ARCTURUS
Arcturus is an orange giant and is classed as a type K star. It is 36 light-years away and has a magnitude of 0.2.

- ● Type O
- ● Type B
- ○ Type A
- ○ Type F
- ○ Type G
- ◐ Type K
- ● Type M

Chart of spectral classes from O (the hottest) to M (the coolest).

SIRIUS
This type A star appears bright because it is just 8.6 light-years away. However, its absolute magnitude is only 1.4.

DATABANK

Q What is the most distant star that can be observed by astronomers?

A A supernova in the galaxy AC 118 was found to be 5 billion light-years away.

Q Which star has the greatest absolute magnitude in our galaxy, the Milky Way?

A Cygnus OB2 number 12 has an absolute magnitude of approximately −10.

RIGEL
A massive blue variable star, Rigel is classed as a type B. It is 900 light-years away and has a magnitude of −8.1.

ALDEBARAN
The orange-red giant Aldebaran is 68 light-years from us. A type K star, it shines with a magnitude of −0.3.

THE SUN

The sun is the solar system's power plant, generating huge amounts of heat and light energy. In the scale of the universe, the sun is not particularly large or powerful, but it is the only star scientists have been able to study in detail.

Structure

Like all stars, the sun is a huge ball of hot gas. Research and probes show that it has an incredibly hot core where the energy is generated. The energy flows outward through the radiation zone and into the next layer, the convection zone, then out to the surface. The sun's surface is called the photosphere. It is about 250–310 miles thick and consists of constantly churning gases. The middle region of the sun's atmosphere is called the chromosphere. It is approximately 5,950 miles deep with temperature ranges from 7,230°F at the bottom to over 90,000°F at the top. Above the chromosphere is the sun's outer atmosphere, called the corona—a glowing halo that extends for several million miles into space.

In 1998, NASA sent the *TRACE* probe to study the sun's corona and photosphere.

Solar flare bursts above corona (outer atmosphere)

Chromosphere (middle atmosphere)

Solar flare

Photosphere (surface)

Sunspot

SOLAR FLARE
A solar flare is a violent explosion over a sunspot, which sends huge amounts of radiation into space.

Photosphere

Photosphere (sun's surface)

Convection zone

Radiation zone

Core or solar interior

Radiation zone

Convection zone

Sunspot

STRUCTURE
The sun is made up of several layers of different temperatures. At its center is the nuclear furnace that makes up its core. While only 2 percent of the sun's volume, the core accounts for 60 percent of its mass.

Solar Furnace

The sun's energy is generated at its core. Extremely high temperatures cause thermonuclear fusion, where the nuclei (core particles) of hydrogen atoms collide and form helium atoms, releasing vast amounts of energy in the form of heat and light. More than 600 million tons of hydrogen are converted into helium every second. The core's temperature rages at 27 million°F. Light and heat energy flow out from the core in waves through the radiation zone and into the convection zone. There, violent churning motions throw the energy out to the visible surface of the sun and on into space.

The sun blasts out seven million tons of material every second. This stream of particles is called the solar wind.

DATABANK

Q Is radiation from the sun dangerous to us?

A Yes. Luckily, ozone in our atmosphere prevents most radiation from reaching Earth.

Q What is a sunspot?

A A dark area on the surface of the sun, which is slightly cooler than the rest of the planet.

ULYSSES
The space probe *Ulysses*, launched in 1990, studies the solar wind and the magnetic field above the sun's poles.

Solar Eclipses

An eclipse is when one planet or satellite blocks out some or all of another. A solar eclipse occurs when the moon's orbit takes it in front of the earth, blocking part or all of the sun from view for a short period. Sometimes the moon only covers part of the sun—this is called a partial eclipse. Total eclipses are rarer, and only a narrow stretch of the earth's surface sees the sun blocked out completely. The total eclipse of August 1999 occupied a 62-mile-wide corridor stretching from the northern Atlantic Ocean, across southwestern England, central Europe, and on into the Middle East and India. Eclipses in 2001 and 2002 will both occur in southern Africa.

When the moon is at its greatest distance from earth, it is too small to cover the sun completely during an eclipse.

DIAMOND
For just a few seconds either side of a total eclipse, a sudden gleam of bright light appears between the mountains of the moon. This stunning sight is referred to as the diamond ring.

GRADES OF SHADOW
During an eclipse, the moon casts a shadow with a dark center, the umbra, surrounded by a lighter area, the penumbra.

FACTS AND FIGURES

The sun's diameter is 870,000 mi. It makes one rotation every 25.4 Earth days.

The sun's mass is 330,000 times greater than Earth's. Its core is about 27 times bigger than Earth.

The number of sunspots rises and falls in eleven-year cycles. The spots move from the poles to the center.

The sun is about 5 billion years old. It will continue to shine for another 5 billion years before it starts to die.

The sun's outer layer consists of 73 percent hydrogen gas, 25 percent helium, and 2 percent other elements.

Just one square centimeter of the sun's surface shines with the brightness of over 230,000 candles.

Sun

Sunlight

Moon's orbit

Earth

Moon

Umbra

Penumbra

Total eclipse

Partial eclipse

BIRTH AND LIFE OF STARS

Just like people, stars are born, live, and die. The difference is that a star's life span is measured in billions of years. New stars are always being born, and scientists are just beginning to understand how.

The cloud of dust and gas found within a nebula may sometimes be the remains of a dead star.

 ## Star Birth

Most stars are born within a huge cloud of gas and dust called a nebula. Space holds millions of nebulae, and they can be observed from Earth when they reflect light from nearby stars. Stars are born when forces within the nebula, such as the pull of the gas's gravity or a shock wave caused by a nearby star explosion, make the cloud of gas and dust shrink and become hotter. As it does so, it breaks up into smaller clumps, each of which may eventually form a star.

 ## Protostars

As the clumps of gas shrink, they form what is called a protostar. This is a baby star that has not started generating energy in its core by nuclear fusion. The shrinking cloud of gas starts to spin around faster and faster. As its speed increases, it becomes a disk shape. The center, or core, of the protostar becomes increasingly dense (compact) and hot until nuclear fusion is finally triggered. The energy produced helps to blow much of the disk of gas away, leaving the new star shining brightly.

CAUGHT IN THE ACT
This pillar of gas and dust is part of the vast Eagle Nebula. Baby stars emerge from the tips at the edge of the cloud.

FACTS AND FIGURES

The Orion Nebula is over 50 light-years across. Scientists have found more than 150 protostars within it.

Algol is an eclipsing variable star where an eclipse occurs once every 2.9 days and lasts for ten hours.

Eta Carinae is an eruptive variable star first discovered in 1677 by English astronomer Edmund Halley.

The first drawing of a nebula was made by Dutch astronomer Christiaan Huygens in 1656.

Mira is a pulsating variable star, which shines at magnitudes that vary between 2.0 and 10.1.

One of the youngest known stars is IRAS4. Astronomers believe it is thousands, rather than millions, of years old.

OUT OF DUST
Here a cloud of gas and dust breaks away from the main nebula. Slowly, the knot of matter gathers together in a disk. As the disk spins, it heats up until a nuclear reaction takes place—a new star is born.

Nebula —a swirling cloud of dust and gas

A dense knot of gas and dust breaks away

LIFE CYCLE
Stars evolve from clouds of dust and gas.
Although born in a similar manner, they
can die in different ways (see pages 28–29).

Long Life

The period of a star's life when it is
shining continuously is called its main
sequence. Most stars astronomers have
observed, including the sun, are somewhere
within their main sequence. Main sequence stars
generate energy by nuclear reactions in their core
that convert hydrogen into helium. How long a star's
main sequence lasts depends on the mass of the star
and how much hydrogen fuel the star contains.

A star's temperature and brightness
remain stable during its main sequence—
about 90 percent of its life span.

MAIN SEQUENCE
For a star the size of our sun,
the main sequence lifetime will
last for about 10 billion years
before the star starts to die.

Variable Stars

Some stars appear to shine unevenly and are known as variable stars. Many of these are really
part of a binary star system where the light from one star is blocked out by the other during
an eclipse. Other stars, near the end of their lives, vary their size and temperature
over a regular period. They are called pulsating variables, and their brightness
varies because of violent shifts in their atmospheres. Stars
that brighten and fade without a regular pattern are
called eruptive variables.

ON AND OFF
A variable star's
brightness varies
because of the
pull and push
of gravity and
pressure in its
outer layers.

The disklike
protostar starts
to spin

Nuclear
reactions get
under way

A young star
burns brightly

DEATH OF STARS

A star may exist for billions of years, but it will not last forever. Eventually, it starts to die. Stars die in a variety of ways and leave behind different legacies, from red giants and white dwarfs to incredibly dense black holes and cataclysmic explosions.

The Beginning of the End

For most stars, the end comes when they begin to use up their hydrogen fuel. A small star, like our sun, then swells up, to become a red giant. Its core continues to burn, using helium as fuel. In some cases, the red giant throws off its outer atmosphere, which becomes what is called a planetary nebula. The core cools and condenses to become a white dwarf, which shines until all its heat radiates away. Stars much larger than our sun contract after they use up their fuel and absorb all the energy instead of giving it off. As the energy is exhausted, the mass of the star increases and, unable to resist the force of gravity, it explodes in a supernova.

When a star explodes in a supernova, it shines more brightly than all the other stars in the galaxy put together.

RED GIANT
At maximum size, a red giant is up to 1,000 times the size of our sun. However, its dense core may only be the size of Earth.

CINDERS
Over billions of years, a white dwarf cools. Eventually, it will shrink to a dark cinder and no longer produce light.

Neutrons and Black Holes

When a massive star dies, its heavy core may become a neutron star. These are the smallest and densest stars. Neutron stars are made when enormous forces compress the star's atoms, forcing protons and electrons in the atoms to make a solid ball of neutrons. Some stars collapse further and disappear into an amazingly dense point called a singularity. A black hole is the space around a singularity. Scientists cannot see a black hole, but they can detect one through its effects.

A black hole is the densest object in the universe. Its gravitational pull is so tremendous even light cannot escape.

POSTSUPERNOVA
The Crab Nebula is a cloud of dust left over from a supernova that was witnessed over China in A.D. 1054.

FACTS AND FIGURES

The first 10 seconds of a supernova produce 100 times more energy than our sun generates in 10 billion years.

If Earth were compressed into solid neutrons, like a neutron star, it would be a ball only 197 ft. in diameter.

A pinhead of solid neutrons would weigh at least as much as two enormous supertanker ships.

When the sun becomes a red giant, it will swell in size to about 30 times its present diameter.

The gas swirling toward a black hole heats up to temperatures as high as 180 million°F.

GIANT STAR DEATH
Blue giants are among the largest and hottest stars in the universe. When they run out of fuel, they usually explode.

SPINNING TOP
Pulsars spin at different speeds, but astronomers believe they all gradually slow down as they run out of energy.

Pulsars

British radio astronomer Jocelyn Bell thought she may have discovered signals from an extraterrestrial intelligence when she monitored a regular series of radio pulses received by the Cambridge radio telescope in 1967. What the scientist had encountered was a pulsar, a rapidly spinning neutron star. Pulsars send out energy in the form of light and radio waves as the star spins around. If Earth is in the path of the beam, then the pulsar's beam appears to blink on and off, like a rotating lighthouse light. Most pulsars flash between five times a second and once every two seconds.

Over 700 pulsars have been discovered so far. The slowest spinners take over 5 seconds to complete a revolution.

GAS THIEF
Many stars come in pairs. If one star dies and collapses into a black hole, it may drag in gas from the other. As the living star's gas spirals into the black hole, it gives off X rays, which can reach Earth.

INTERGALACTIC FLASHER
As a pulsar spins, escaping electrons are channeled into a beam of radiation and light by the star's massive magnetic field.

GIVE AWAY
Scientists study the X rays given off by a black hole's activity in order to locate the hole's exact position in space.

DATABANK

INPUT

Q What is the speed of the fastest-spinning pulsar found so far?

Q Where do scientists think the nearest black hole to Earth is?

Q Will our own sun die, and if so, when will it happen?

Q Could a human possibly travel in and out of a black hole?

OUTPUT

A In 1982, experts found a pulsar that spins 642 times a second.

A There may be a black hole within our own galaxy, the Milky Way.

A Yes, it will start to run out of hydrogen in about 5 billion years.

A As far as scientists can tell, nothing escapes from a black hole.

EXPANDING UNIVERSE

The universe consists of space and everything within it. It is unbelievably huge and appears to be getting bigger. There are many ideas about how the universe was born, but the most widely accepted theory among scientists is the Big Bang theory.

IN THE BEGINNING
The Big Bang created enough energy to make all the matter in the universe. The universe then began to expand.

EARLY DAYS
As the swiftly expanding universe cooled, the forces that governed it, such as gravity and nuclear reactions, separated out. Atoms did not form for at least 300,000 years after the Big Bang.

 ## The Big Bang

The Big Bang theory suggests that the entire universe started more than 12 billion years ago. It began in a minute point when some form of gigantic explosion started the process of forming matter, time, and space. No one knows what caused the Big Bang, but it is believed that the explosion was followed by cosmic inflation in which incredible forces were generated. In the smallest fraction of a second, the universe grew from smaller than an atom to bigger than a galaxy. Since then, it has continued to expand rapidly.

OUT OF NOTHINGNESS
The Big Bang occurred within the tiniest fraction of time. Nothing occurred before it—not even time or space.

FACTS AND FIGURES

Edwin Hubble discovered the universe was expanding in 1929. The Hubble Space Telescope is named after him.

The idea of the Big Bang was first detailed by Belgian priest Bernard Lemaître in the 1920s.

The Big Bang explosion would have generated temperatures in excess of 10 octillion°F.

The communications satellite *Telstar* was the first device to detect possible radiation left over from the Big Bang.

The phrase "Big Bang" was first used by the British astronomer Fred Hoyle in a radio program.

 ## Spaced Out

The Cosmic Background Explorer (COBE) telescope found signs of the Big Bang in the universe's background radiation.

Through much research, we have learned that the universe is becoming larger and larger every day. Three billion years ago, for example, galaxy clusters were 25 percent closer than they are today. Although the universe is increasing in size, it is not expanding into anything. Space itself is expanding, carrying clusters of galaxies with it. The force of gravity is the only counter to this expansion. Gravity is strong enough between planets and galaxies to keep them together. The gravity that stars and galaxies exert, however, does not appear to be enough to stop the universe itself from expanding, so the space between galaxies increases.

Redshift

Redshift is a term used to describe how certain galaxies in the universe are moving away from us. We know that light travels in waves, and the color of light depends on its wavelength. When a galaxy moves away from us, light waves from it are stretched out and are red in color—the light waves are said to be "redshifted." If the galaxy is moving toward us, the light waves appear squashed together or "blueshifted." Astronomers analyze a galaxy's redshift to measure the speed at which it travels. The detection of a redshift in almost all galaxies that astronomers have studied is seen by many as proof that the universe is expanding. We cannot see redshift with the naked eye, but we can detect and measure it using an instrument called a spectrograph.

REDSHIFT
This illustration shows distant galaxies redshifting. By studying redshift, scientists have calculated that the galaxies are moving away from us at speeds of thousands of miles per second.

The American astronomer Vesto Melvin Slipher was the first to observe a redshift in a galaxy, in 1912.

EVER BIGGER
The universe continued to expand with such energy that parts of it are still moving away from each other to this day.

GALAXIES
Some 300 million years after the Big Bang, the universe consisted of voids surrounded by filaments of gas. Dense clumps of gas started to pull together, and, after one billion years, formed galaxies.

COSMOLOGY

Cosmology looks at the big questions about the universe. It deals less with the makeup of individual planets and stars, and more with how the universe started, how it has evolved, and how it will end—if at all.

 ## Ever-expanding Universe

No one is certain whether the universe will last forever or will end in the distant future. Some astronomers believe that the universe is not only expanding, but will continue to do so. This is called the open universe theory. When something has a definite beginning and end—either time or space—it is called finite. An ever-expanding universe would be infinite; it would exist over all space and for all time. However, the stars and galaxies within the universe may slowly die, leaving a huge, cold, empty space.

The open universe theory is sometimes called the Big Bore theory because there is nothing exciting to describe.

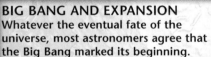

BIG BANG AND EXPANSION
Whatever the eventual fate of the universe, most astronomers agree that the Big Bang marked its beginning.

SLOW DOWN
In the closed universe model, there is enough mass in the universe for gravity to slow the expansion. Eventually the expansion will be brought to a halt, and the universe will begin to contract.

 ## Closed Universe

In the closed model of the universe, scientists believe that gravity between galaxies and clusters will eventually prevent the universe from expanding any farther. The galaxies may then be dragged back toward each other until they collide, forming a giant black hole. This prediction of a violent ending for the universe is called the Big Crunch theory. Many cosmologists believe that the gravitational pull that will drag all the galaxies back together will be provided by the huge quantity of invisible matter, known as dark matter (see right), that holds the universe together.

By the time a closed universe slows to a halt, our own solar system will be long dead.

Some cosmologists believe that a new universe could emerge from the black hole created by the Big Crunch.

DATABANK

INPUT

Q How big is the universe?

Q If the Big Crunch theory is correct, how long does the universe have to run?

Q How much of the universe could be made up of dark matter?

OUTPUT

A We know that the most distant galaxies from us are at least ten billion light-years away.

A The Big Crunch, if it happens, will be billions of years into the future.

A As much as 90 percent.

BIG BORE
The open universe model has the universe expanding forever. However, stars and galaxies will eventually grow cold and die.

CONTRACTING
Galaxies and stars, pulled by gravity, start moving back toward each other. Space begins to heat up.

BIG CRUNCH
As the universe contracts, black holes at the center of galaxies merge to form one massive black hole, sucking in all matter.

REBIRTH
If a new universe emerged from the Big Crunch, it could feature different laws of physics to the current universe.

Dark matter may be made up of something called WIMPS—Weakly Interacting Massive Particles.

Dark Matter

One key question that perplexes cosmologists is the missing mass of the universe. Only a small part of the universe is visible to our eyes with optical telescopes or detected by scientific instruments, but the gravitational pull on nearby galaxies indicates that there is invisible matter out there. It is called dark matter, but no one knows what it is made of. There are plenty of ideas of what dark matter might be, including black holes, very faint stars, brown dwarfs (objects too big to be planets and too small and cold to be stars), cold gas between the stars, or subatomic particles called neutrinos. The amount of dark matter in the universe could have an enormous bearing on how the universe evolved and whether it may, one day, cease to exist.

DARK QUEST
A disused coal mine in Britain is leading the search for dark matter. A detector (A) is placed 3,600 ft. below the surface so that light and cosmic rays (blue lines) are blocked by the rock above. This allows it to pick up dark matter (yellow lines).

A

MILKY WAY

The solar system is the first line of Earth's address. The next line is the group of stars in which the solar system is located—the galaxy known as the Milky Way. It is a fascinating place, although we have studied only a mere fraction of its stars and nebulae.

First Impressions

The Milky Way is a spiral galaxy with several curving arms that extend to form its disklike shape. The Milky Way's center is an oval-shaped bulge, which is about 4,000 light-years thicker than the rest of the galaxy. Although we cannot see the center because it is shrouded in clouds of gas and dust, scientific instruments can penetrate the gloom and give us a hint of what lies inside. The center spins faster than the rest of the galaxy and contains millions of stars, many of them red or yellow, giving the central bulge a distinct, yellowish tinge. Astronomers believe the Milky Way's center may contain a black hole.

If the solar system were the size of a coffee mug, the Milky Way would be the size of North America.

SLIVER OF SPACE
This infrared image removes intervening dust and gas to show that the Milky Way, when viewed from the side, is a thin disk.

Features of the Milky Way

Although the view of much of the Milky Way is obstructed, astronomers have identified many different features, including a large number of nebulae. The illustration at the bottom left of this page shows some of the sun's neighbors in the galaxy. These are: 1. Cone Nebula; 2. Rosette Nebula; 3. Orion Nebula; 4. Lagoon Nebula; 5. Our solar system; 6. California Nebula; 7. Trifid Nebula; 8. Vela Supernova Remnant; 9. North America Nebula. Each of these nebulae is in the process of creating new stars.

A galactic year is the time it takes the solar system to orbit the Milky Way's center.

BITE OF MILKY WAY
While some galaxies appear to have no nebulae, and therefore no potential for new stars, the Milky Way has many.

Birth of the Milky Way

Even at a speed of 150 mi. per second, the sun takes 220 million years to orbit the center of the Milky Way.

Although a relatively small galaxy, the Milky Way has a mass equal to about 1 trillion suns.

Light takes 12 hours to cross the solar system, but takes 100,000 years to cross the Milky Way.

The nearest galaxy to the Milky Way, the Sagittarius galaxy, is being ripped apart by the Milky Way's gravity.

Gravity is pulling the Milky Way and Andromeda galaxies together at a speed of 186 mi. per second.

The total mass of all the stars in the Milky Way is equal to about 200 million of our suns.

The spiral galaxy that is the Milky Way formed some five billion years after the Big Bang. A massive cloud of hydrogen and helium gas started to collapse in on itself under the influence of gravity. The gas at the center was pulled tightly together until it was dense enough to begin forming stars. This protogalaxy started spinning and, as its speed increased, the outer area flattened into a disk shape. Gradually, key features of the Milky Way formed, such as its wispy, tendrillike arms. Scientists studying the birth of other galaxies believe that if they spin slowly during formation, they become irregular or elliptical galaxies.

The word *galaxy* comes from the Greek word for milk. Ancient Greeks believed the Milky Way was milk from the gods.

SPINNING CLOUD
A slowly spinning mass of gas collapses and draws matter toward its center to form stars. It starts to spin faster.

FRESH GALAXY
The galaxy is now fully formed. The arms contain many nebulae and continue to produce new stars.

A SHAPE EMERGES
Gas clouds merge within the swirling disk, and the force of gravity attracts more material. Arms begin to take shape.

MILLIONS OF MILKY WAYS
This photograph shows just a tiny portion of space. Even so, it is clear that there are countless other galaxies out there.

The Magellanic Clouds are small, irregular galaxies that orbit the Milky Way once every 1.5 billion years.

DATABANK

INPUT	OUTPUT
Q How many stars are there in the Milky Way?	**A** Around 200 billion.
Q How did the Milky Way get its spiral shape?	**A** Its spinning motion has flattened it into a disk shape.
Q When did we discover that the Milky Way was a spiral galaxy?	**A** American astronomer William Morgan proved this in 1951.
Q Do we know where the exact center of the Milky Way is?	**A** Yes. Astronomers place it in an area called Sagittarius A.

GALAXIES

How many galaxies does the universe contain? Ten thousand? Half a million? Astronomers estimate that a staggering 100 billion galaxies in numerous shapes and sizes exist across space, gathered into clusters.

Galaxy Types

In 1924, Edwin Hubble proved that other galaxies existed beyond the Milky Way. Astronomers catalog galaxies in several ways, but the most important factor is their basic shape. More than half of all galaxies observed are elliptical, which means round or oval. The other common shapes are spiral galaxies, like the Milky Way, and barred spirals, which have a central bar of material running through their hub or center. A fourth type, called irregular galaxies, include those that don't fit into any of the above classes. Irregular galaxies tend to have no obvious shape and are rich in gas and dust. Spiral and barred spiral galaxies are further classified into four groups, according to how large their centers are and how tight their arms wind around the center. Elliptical galaxies are divided into eight different classes from E0 to E7. E0 galaxies are almost ball shaped, while E7 galaxies resemble flattened ovals.

SPIRAL AND BARRED SPIRAL
Spiral galaxies (left) have loosely or tightly wound arms. Barred spiral galaxies (above) have a central bar between the spirals.

Elliptical galaxies seem to have no nebulae, which means they cannot form new stars.

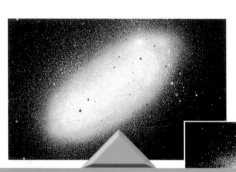

ELLIPTICAL AND IRREGULAR
Elliptical galaxies (above) range in shape from ovals to spheres. Irregular galaxies (right) have no recognizable shape.

Active Galaxies

A small number of galaxies have very luminous cores that pump energy and material into space. These are known as active galaxies and are widely varied, including radio galaxies, quasars, and Seyfert galaxies. Quasars are among the most powerful objects in the universe and also the most distant from Earth. Astronomers believe that a huge black hole lies in an active galaxy's center. As gas and, possibly, complete stars are sucked into the black hole, huge amounts of energy in the form of radio waves, infrared, light, and X rays are sent into space. Earth's nearest quasar is PKS 2349-01, 1.5 million light-years away.

Energy given off

 Black hole

Matter spins around rapidly as it is sucked in

QUASAR
A quasar may contain a black hole. As it draws in matter, the black hole ejects huge amounts of energy.

FACTS AND FIGURES

Malin 1 is the largest galaxy recorded. It is thought to be 1,000 times larger than the Milky Way.

Dwarf elliptical galaxies are believed to be the most common type of galaxy in the entire universe.

The first quasar ever to be discovered was by the Dutch astronomer Maarten Schmidt in 1963.

Irregular galaxies are thought to have been pulled out of shape by the gravity of other nearby galaxies.

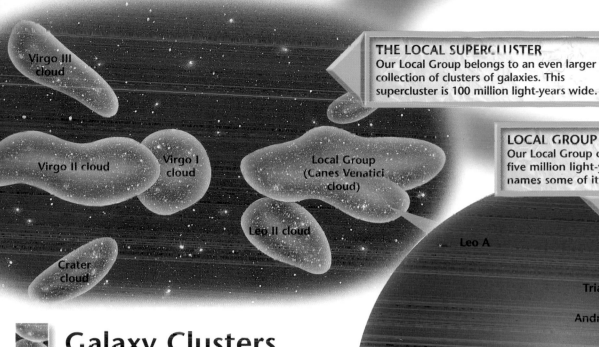

THE LOCAL SUPERCLUSTER
Our Local Group belongs to an even larger collection of clusters of galaxies. This supercluster is 100 million light-years wide.

Virgo III cloud

Virgo II cloud

Virgo I cloud

Local Group (Canes Venatici cloud)

Leo II cloud

Crater cloud

LOCAL GROUP
Our Local Group can be shown as a sphere five million light-years across. This image names some of its main galaxies.

Leo A

Triangulum (M33)

Andromeda

Milky Way

GR8

Pisces

NGC 6822

Galaxy Clusters

Galaxies exist in larger groups, called clusters, held together by the pull of gravity. Our own galaxy, the Milky Way, is the second largest of at least 30 galaxies that form a cluster called the Local Group (right), which can be pictured as a sphere five million light-years wide. The Local Group contains a range of fascinating galaxies, such as Andromeda (the largest), Triangulam (the third largest), and smaller Pisces. The galaxy Leo A is the most distant member of the group. The most common types of galaxy in the group are the approximately 15 dwarf galaxies.

The Andromeda galaxy in our Local Group is the most distant object visible to the naked eye.

M100
The M100 galaxy is the brightest spiral galaxy in the Virgo Cluster. It is 20 times more luminous than our own sun. This computer enhanced image was taken by the Hubble Space Telescope.

 ## Supercluster

Although huge, our Local Group is an outlying and minor part of a massive collection of galaxies known as the Coma-Virgo Supercluster (see top). As well as our Local Group of galaxies, the supercluster holds ten other clouds of galaxies. In total, the supercluster measures around 100 million light-years across. At its center lies the Virgo Cluster. This large and fascinating group of more than 2,000 galaxies is over 50 million light-years away. It is often referred to as a galactic zoo, because it contains examples of all the major galaxy types. Its proximity to Earth and its bright, well-spaced galaxies make it easy to observe.

The Virgo cluster's M87 galaxy ejects a continuous jet of gassy material 5,000 light-years in length.

EARLY SKYWATCHING

Skywatching is not new. From images and positions of stars painted on cave walls 10,000 years ago, we know that people have always been fascinated with the skies.

 ## Ancient Skywatchers

Many ancient civilizations studied the night sky—from the Babylonians, Egyptians, and Polynesians to cultures in central and South America. Archaeologists have unearthed a number of artifacts that show star maps and record the position of the sun, moon, and Earth.

The Chinese astronomers Hsi and Ho were executed in 2137 B.C. when they failed to predict an eclipse.

Early skywatchers also observed comets with sparkling tails and meteors or shooting stars apparently falling from the sky. All over the world, ancient astronomers observed points of light that appeared to move among the stars. They called these objects planets, meaning wanderers. Their present names are taken from those of the Roman gods: Jupiter, the king of the gods; Mars, the god of war; Mercury, the messenger of the gods; Venus, the goddess of love and beauty; and Saturn, the god of agriculture.

EARLY OBSERVATORY
Many people believe that Stonehenge is a calender and was used to mark the position of the midsummer sunrise.

DATABANK

Q What is the Dresden Codex?

A It is an Ancient Mayan text from South America showing details of the Moon and Venus.

Q Who was the first woman to be connected with astronomy?

A Hyspatria of Alexandria taught astronomy and mathematics 1,600 years ago.

HEAVENS ABOVE
The ancient Egyptians studied the sun, moon, and stars and based many of their festivals on the movement of these bodies.

STAR MAP
Many remnants of Chinese star maps have been found. They show parts of the night sky mapped in great detail. This map shows the Big Dipper, which is part of the constellation Ursa Major (Great Bear).

 ## Chinese Stargazers

In many early cultures, the study and knowledge of the stars was firmly entwined with religion. The incredible sights in the night sky were believed to be gods or spirits in action. The Chinese have a long history of recording astronomical phenomena. In the past they believed that earthly events were influenced by what happened in the heavens. Historians have found records of eclipses from 1,000–2,000 B.C., as well as records kept by the Chinese astronomer Shih-shen, in which he cataloged 809 stars, around 600 B.C.

Ancient Greeks

The ancient Greeks took astronomy very seriously, turning it into a science with Hipparchus and Ptolemy among the most important Greek astronomers. Hipparchus constructed the first in-depth star chart, in which he named around 850 stars. He also predicted the positions of the planets and attempted to estimate the distance of the moon from Earth. The astronomer and geographer Ptolemy is most famous for his theory that the earth was the center of the entire universe. The Ptolemaic view portrayed all the planets, including the sun and moon, revolving around the earth with the night sky made up of a giant sphere of never-changing stars, which also revolved around Earth. His views were accepted until the 1500s and 1600s.

PTOLEMY
Ptolemy (A.D. 85–165) lived in Alexandria, Egypt, during the time of Roman occupation. His ideas were taken up by the Byzantines—the successors to the Roman Empire—and later the Arabs.

SELF-CENTERED
Ptolemy's view of an earth-centered universe was based on the ideas of earlier great scientists such as Aristotle and Plato.

DANGEROUS IDEA?
Many people thought that Copernicus' idea of a sun-centered universe directly challenged the Bible.

The Copernican Revolution

Ptolemy's view of Earth as the center of the universe held sway for 1,500 years. It was first challenged by a Polish monk and astronomer, Nikolas Copernicus. His theory, which placed the sun at the center of the universe, has been proven wrong, but he was correct that the planets orbit the Sun. Copernicus' views clashed with the Church, which believed in Ptolemy's model. It took the work of astronomers like Tycho Brahe, Johannes Kepler, and Galileo before Copernicus' view of the solar system was accepted.

MULTITALENTED
Copernicus was not only an astronomer, he was also a monk, bailiff, judge, tax collector, and physician.

In the 1600s, Danish astronomer Tycho Brahe calculated the length of an Earth year to within one second.

FACTS AND FIGURES

The Dogon tribe of West Africa could see Saturn's rings without the aid of a telescope.

Ptolemy's famous book, the *Almagest,* is a collection of 13 books that were translated by Arab scholars.

Over one hundred stars still carry the names originally given to them many centuries ago.

Native Americans used sighting the Pleiades group of stars as a way of testing a warrior's eyesight

Tycho Brahe lost most of his nose in a duel. He wore a false silver, gold, and wax nose for the rest of his life.

STARGAZING

From Earth, the night sky appears to be a filled with a confusing array of stars. Groups of stars, called constellations, act as a kind of road map and help us navigate through the heavens.

NIGHT VISION
It takes about 30 minutes for our eyes to become accustomed to the night sky so that we can see objects more clearly.

The Sky at Night

Beginners usually find skywatching confusing at first because the stars appear to move each night. Although stars seem to keep their positions relative to each other, they appear in a slightly different place each evening and gently "drift" across the sky during the night. This movement is largely caused by Earth's passage around the sun. One tricky obstacle for the astronomer is light pollution. This is caused by city lights, which spread their glow across parts of the night sky, drowning out fainter stars. On a clear night, stranger sights may be found among the stars, planets, and galaxies on show. Meteor showers and comets sometimes appear, while people living near the North or South pole may be treated to an aurora. These wonderful light shows occur when particles from the sun are attracted to Earth's magnetic poles.

Inexperienced skywatchers commonly report Venus as an unidentified flying object (UFO).

Celestial Sphere

Originally a constellation was regarded as a star system, but now it refers to an area of the sky. The idea of constellations can be confusing, so astronomers refer to the celestial sphere—an imaginary sphere surrounding Earth with all the stars inside. The constellations are dotted around the sphere's surface, which is usually divided into a grid to allow stargazers to easily locate a particular area.

The stars within a constellation may not belong to the same galaxy or even the same galaxy cluster.

SKY MAP
The celestial sphere is an imaginary globe surrounding Earth with its north and south poles aligned with those of Earth. It is a convenient way to map three dimensional space from Earth.

Different Skies

The celestial sphere is divided into two halves, known as hemispheres (see below). People living in the Northern Hemisphere can only see northern constellations and a few stars from the south, while people in the south see the opposite. Additionally, Earth's orbit and rotation mean that only a few of each hemisphere's constellations can be seen at any one time.

The International Astronomical Union decides the names of constellations and new stars and galaxies.

Pegasus

Phoenix

Northern

Southern

Ursa Major

Leo

Scorpio

Hercules

Crux (Southern Cross)

Libra

Astrologers believe that the movement of planets within the zodiac has a strong influence on human affairs

 # DATABANK

Q What is a planisphere?

A It is a circular map of the stars showing where they will be on a certain day or at a certain time.

Q Who discovered the first constellations?

A The Babylonians are believed to have found the first constellations before 2000 B.C.

 # The Zodiac

One band of 12 constellations runs right around the celestial sphere. Known as the zodiac, these constellations feature the names of the star signs used in astrology. The moon, sun, and all of the planets—except Pluto—travel across the sky within this band of stars. The sun appears to spend roughly a month in each constellation of the zodiac.

SIGNS OF THE ZODIAC
1. Capricorn; 2. Aquarius; 3. Pisces; 4. Aries;
5. Taurus; 6. Gemini; 7. Cancer; 8. Leo; 9. Virgo; 10. Libra; 11. Scorpio; 12. Sagittarius.

TELESCOPES

Until the 1600s, people relied on the naked eye to view the skies. The invention of optical telescopes has enabled astronomers to peer into the far reaches of space.

Refracting Telescopes

Dutch opticians exhibited the first telescopes in 1608–9. They placed two glass lenses in a tube and found that distant objects appeared closer than before. The lenses bent, or refracted, the light and enlarged the image. Italian astronomer Galileo quickly latched on to the new invention and built a telescope with 30 times the magnification of the human eye. He used it to study the night sky. However, larger lenses are difficult to build because if the glass lens is over 3 feet in diameter, its weight can cause the lens to bend and become distorted.

EARLY TELESCOPE
Early refracting telescopes were very long in order to give the viewer a clear image of the stars.

Large lenses can suffer from chromatic aberration—rainbow colors appearing around the edges of an image.

The world's largest refracting telescope is at Yerkes Observatory, Wisconsin. Built in 1897, its aperture is 3.5 ft.

Refracting telescope

- Light waves
- Eyepiece
- Objective lens

TELESCOPES
While refractors use lenses to enlarge images, reflectors rely on curved mirrors to magnify light waves.

Reflecting telescope

- Flat mirror
- Curved mirror
- Light waves
- Eyepiece

Reflecting Telescopes

To see farther and in more detail, bigger telescopes were required with more light-gathering power than refracting telescopes. Reflecting telescopes, or reflectors, first introduced in 1668, now comprise all of the world's largest telescopes. These use large, ultrasmooth mirrors—easier to build and support than large lenses—to collect light. Our eyes have an opening, or aperture, of up to .25 inches to let light in. Reflecting telescopes can have apertures measured in feet. Reflecting telescopes send their images to computers and scientific instruments, which divide the light into different wavelengths, or to a charge coupled device (CCD)—a powerful, high-resolution form of digital camera.

HOMEMADE
William Herschel (1738–1822) built a large reflecting telescope in his backyard. The opening, or aperture, was 4 ft. wide. The viewer stood on a platform below this in order to study very faint objects.

LOOKING UP
This astronomical telescope on Palomar Mountain in California has a reflector over 16 ft. in diameter. Called the George Ellery Hale Telescope, it was the world's largest reflecting telescope from 1947 until 1970.

In 1838, telescopes allowed astronomers to measure the distance from Earth to a star for the first time.

Hubble

Telescopes placed in orbit around Earth overcome the obstacle of Earth's thick atmosphere and allow uninterrupted viewing of the universe beyond our solar system. The Hubble Space Telescope is the most famous example. Orbiting at 378 miles above Earth's surface, Hubble has made vital discoveries that have changed what we know about space. In 1995, for example, Hubble photographed the birth of a star in the Eagle Nebula and produced a view of galaxies up to 10 billion light-years away. Hubble's solar panels generate the electricity to power its reflecting telescope and other instruments that allow it to see infrared and ultraviolet waves being emitted from distant stars and galaxies.

FARSIGHTED
Launched in 1990, the Hubble Space Telescope is powered by solar panels 40 ft. long and 8 ft. wide. Its observations are sent down to radio telescopes on Earth where scientists can decipher them.

To be launched in 2009, the Next Generation Space Telescope will be 400 times as powerful as any ground telescope.

FACTS AND FIGURES

The Very Large Telescope, under construction in Chile, will be able to spot a small insect 6,200 mi. away.

Sir Isaac Newton invented the first reflecting telescope in 1668. It had a mirror made of copper, tin, and arsenic.

The observatory at Lowell, Arizona, opened in the 1890s. It was from here that Pluto was discovered.

In 1999, the Hubble Space Telescope detected the most powerful explosion ever observed.

Reflectors must have smooth mirrors. The Gemini telescope's 26 ft. mirror was polished for over a year.

The mirror on the Large Binocular Telescope (LBT) on Mt. Graham, Arizona, weighs over 16 tons.

Observatories

Large optical telescopes are often found with other scientific instruments in a specifically designed installation called an observatory. The first observatories were built by wealthy people with an amateur interest in astronomy. Today, dozens of advanced observatories run by governments and scientific organizations are dotted throughout the world. Most are built at high altitudes away from cities, so that smoke and light pollution does not interfere with the view. Devices called interferometers are used to link telescopes together to build a computer-controlled and more detailed image of a subject. The data collected in just a small number of nights' viewing is frequently enough to keep astronomers busy for many months.

The Lowell Observatory was built by Percival Lowell to investigate his belief that intelligent life existed on Mars.

CLEAR VIEW
At over 7,000 ft. above sea level, La Palma Observatory in the Canary Islands avoids most light and atmospheric pollution.

NON-OPTICAL TELESCOPES

Scientists have learned that visible light is just one of several types of electromagnetic radiation that reach us from space. Radio telescopes and other instruments have been developed to collect information from these sources and peer far beyond the visible universe.

Radio Telescopes

As well as sending out light waves, many objects in space emit radio waves, which are invisible to the human eye or optical telescopes. We have learned how to collect these radio waves in order to detect and learn about objects too distant or not bright enough to be seen with optical telescopes. Most radio telescopes (see left) use a concave (curved inward or bowl-shaped) dish to collect radio waves from space. The radio waves are reflected from the dish to an antenna, which changes them to electric signals. A receiver amplifies (strengthens) the signal. Computers are used to process the signal into images and data, which can be analyzed by radio astronomers.

Reflector dish

Antenna

Tilt

Receiver

Revolving base

Visible light

Infrared radiation—blocked by the atmosphere

Radio waves

Radio telescope

Optical telescope

OPTICAL VERSES RADIO
Radio waves and visible light waves pass through Earth's atmosphere and are picked up by optical and radio telescopes.

RADIO TELESCOPE
Radio telescopes can be moved to follow a particular celestial body's progress across the sky or to view different parts of space.

Amateur U.S. astronomer Grote Reber built one of the first radio telescopes. Some of it was made from car parts.

Single Dishes and Arrays

Unlike optical telescopes, radio telescopes operate 24 hours a day and can still work through thick cloud and air pollution. However, radio waves have less energy than light waves. There are two solutions to this obstacle: build very large dishes to collect enough data, or link many smaller dishes together to form what is called an array. Examples of both single dishes and arrays may be found throughout the world.

WORLD'S LARGEST ARRAY
The Very Large Array (VLA) telescope in New Mexico, has 27 dishes. It simulates the effect of a single dish 17 mi. wide.

The data from the dishes of the Very Large Array is combined to produce one radio image.

Infrared Astronomy

Infrared (heat) waves lie just beyond the visible spectrum of light. Everything in the universe cooler than around 5,400°F emits some infrared radiation. Infrared telescopes on Earth and in space are used to look at the cooler elements of the universe and can detect objects as cold as dust clouds at -330°F. Infrared astronomy has revealed thousands of galaxies never observed before and has also discovered water vapor in space.

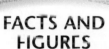

DEEPER VISION
NASA's Infrared Telescope Facility (IRTF) in Hawaii is used to study planet atmospheres and dust clouds in space.

JUPITER REVEALED
The red and yellow bands in this infrared image of Jupiter show the hottest areas of the planet's surface.

DATABANK

Q Who was the first person to detect radio waves from space?

A American Karl Jansky discovered radio waves from space in 1932.

Q What features have radio telescopes discovered about the universe?

A The many finds include quasars, pulsars, and background radiation from the Big Bang.

FACTS AND FIGURES

The world's first professional radio telescope was built at Jodrell Bank, Cheshire, England, in 1947.

Infrared telescopes detected 1,860-mi.-long plumes when comet Shoemaker Levy 9 hit Jupiter in 1994.

An ultraviolet observatory was set up on the moon in 1972 by the crew of the *Apollo 16* lunar mission.

The largest radio telescope dish in the world is the Arecibo dish in Puerto Rico. It is 1,000 ft. in diameter.

The first ultraviolet telescope in space was the Copernicus Satellite telescope, launched in 1972.

Gamma rays are high-energy waves created by radioactive decay and by nuclear reactions in stars.

Checking Out Other Waves

Radio, light, and infrared waves are not the only types of signals we receive from space. Astronomers are also using scientific instruments to detect and measure X rays, gamma rays, and ultraviolet rays in space. Extremely sensitive telescopes are attached to orbiting satellites in space because ultraviolet light, X rays, and gamma rays are absorbed by Earth's atmosphere and do not reach the ground. To track down the hottest stars in the universe, those with temperatures above 18,000°F, astronomers are using ultraviolet telescopes.

RADAR IMAGING
An image of a planet's surface can be recorded by beaming radio waves at it and then interpreting the returning echo.

MICROWAVES
Taken by the *Microwave Limb Sounder* satellite, these images show the movement of water vapor over the Pacific Ocean.

BLAST OFF

Gravity keeps us on Earth. To escape its strong pull and go into space, rockets must travel incredibly fast— over 7 miles per second! This speed is called a rocket's "escape velocity."

WAR—THE MOTHER OF INVENTION
Space rockets evolved from rocket missiles like this German V2, a number of which attacked Britain during World War II.

- Launch escape route
- Command module
- Propulsion engine
- Service module
- Lunar module
- Instrument unit
- **Third stage**
- Liquid oxygen
- 1 rocket engine
- Liquid nitrogen
- **Second stage**
- Liquid oxygen
- 5 rocket engines
- Liquid oxygen
- **First stage**
- Kerosene fuel

Rocket Pioneers

The Chinese fired simple, rocketlike fireworks over 800 years ago, but it wasn't until the 1900s that rockets were used to send objects into space. The Soviet scientist Konstantin Tsiolovsky (1857–1935) was the first to seriously suggest the idea. Development work was performed by many scientists and engineers, including Herman Oberth, Robert H. Goddard, and Wernher von Braun. In 1926 Goddard, a U.S. scientist, became the first to launch a small rocket propelled by liquid fuel. Oberth and von Braun were both Germans who, after World War II, worked on rockets for the U.S. space program, including the Saturn V rocket.

Although rockets deliver humans and planetary probes into space, their main use is to launch commercial satellites.

Multistage Rockets

Single-stage rockets can reach low Earth orbit, but they do not have the power to break completely free of Earth's gravity. The solution has been to build rockets that work in stages. As one stage uses up its fuel and, therefore, power, it separates from the rest of the rocket and falls away. This reduces the weight being carried and allows rockets to carry spacecraft out of low Earth orbits and into space. The two-stage Russian Vostok launcher launched the first satellite into space, *Sputnik 1*, and the first person in space, Yuri Gagarin. These were just two of its 150 missions.

MIGHTY ROCKET
The Saturn V rocket, which was used on the manned moon missions, consisted of three stages, each with its own fuel tank.

FIRST STAGE
As the Saturn V rocket leaves Earth's atmosphere, the first stage falls away to be burned up in the outer atmosphere.

SECOND STAGE
This fires for six minutes, pushing the rocket to 13,600 mph. It is finally jettisoned 118 miles above Earth.

Reusable Rockets

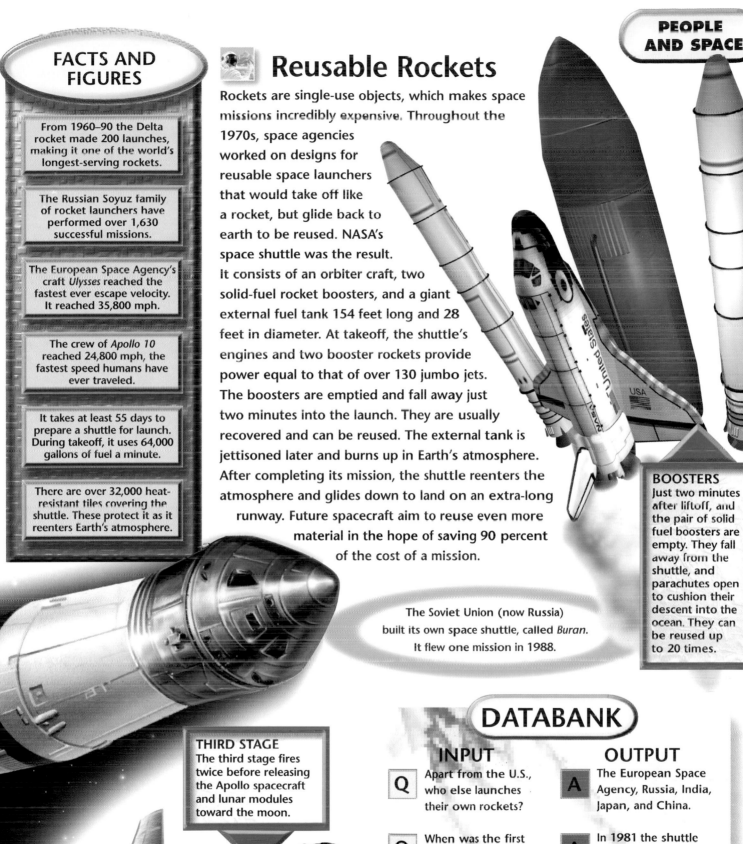

Rockets are single-use objects, which makes space missions incredibly expensive. Throughout the 1970s, space agencies worked on designs for reusable space launchers that would take off like a rocket, but glide back to earth to be reused. NASA's space shuttle was the result. It consists of an orbiter craft, two solid-fuel rocket boosters, and a giant external fuel tank 154 feet long and 28 feet in diameter. At takeoff, the shuttle's engines and two booster rockets provide power equal to that of over 130 jumbo jets. The boosters are emptied and fall away just two minutes into the launch. They are usually recovered and can be reused. The external tank is jettisoned later and burns up in Earth's atmosphere. After completing its mission, the shuttle reenters the atmosphere and glides down to land on an extra-long runway. Future spacecraft aim to reuse even more material in the hope of saving 90 percent of the cost of a mission.

FACTS AND FIGURES

From 1960–90 the Delta rocket made 200 launches, making it one of the world's longest-serving rockets.

The Russian Soyuz family of rocket launchers have performed over 1,630 successful missions.

The European Space Agency's craft *Ulysses* reached the fastest ever escape velocity. It reached 35,800 mph.

The crew of *Apollo 10* reached 24,800 mph, the fastest speed humans have ever traveled.

It takes at least 55 days to prepare a shuttle for launch. During takeoff, it uses 64,000 gallons of fuel a minute.

There are over 32,000 heat-resistant tiles covering the shuttle. These protect it as it reenters Earth's atmosphere.

BOOSTERS
Just two minutes after liftoff, and the pair of solid fuel boosters are empty. They fall away from the shuttle, and parachutes open to cushion their descent into the ocean. They can be reused up to 20 times.

The Soviet Union (now Russia) built its own space shuttle, called *Buran*. It flew one mission in 1988.

THIRD STAGE
The third stage fires twice before releasing the Apollo spacecraft and lunar modules toward the moon.

DATABANK

INPUT

Q Apart from the U.S., who else launches their own rockets?

Q When was the first shuttle launched and what was its name?

Q How many space shuttles have been built by NASA?

OUTPUT

A The European Space Agency, Russia, India, Japan, and China.

A In 1981 the shuttle *Columbia* spent 54 hours in space.

A Six—*Columbia, Atlantis, Challenger, Discovery, Endeavour,* and *Enterprise.*

ARTIFICIAL SATELLITES

Objects sent into orbit are called satellites. Since 1957, over 4,000 satellites have been launched. They perform tasks such as forecasting weather and relaying telephone and TV transmissions all over the world.

 ## Orbiting Earth

All satellites are designed to obtain information of some kind and communicate it back to ground stations on Earth via radio transmitters. Satellites are launched by rocket or carried into space by space shuttles. Once in orbit, satellites must travel at a precise speed that keeps them at a consistent distance from Earth at all times. This prevents the craft from falling back into the atmosphere and being destroyed. Some satellites have tiny jet thrusters on board that make small changes to the satellite's position, keeping it on the correct path.

Some satellites are launched directly from the cargo bay of the space shuttle.

RELEASE
Most satellites are carried into orbit in a rocket. Once it reaches the correct height, the rocket releases, or deploys, the satellite. The rocket falls away from the satellite and cannot be used again.

SUN DRIVEN
Most satellites are powered by batteries charged by solar cells in the wing panels or wrapped around the satellite's body.

DATABANK

Q How many countries have their own satellites?

A Just over 35, including Sweden, Chile, Egypt, and Thailand.

Q Do spy satellites exist?

A Yes. From their orbits hundreds of miles above Earth they can detect objects 4 inches wide.

 ## Triggering the Space Race

Competition between the U.S. and the former Soviet Union led to the space race. The Soviets scored first by launching the first successful artificial satellite, *Sputnik 1*, in October 1957. *Sputnik 1* was a metal ball nearly 2 feet across that orbited the earth once every 96 minutes, sending back radio signals. After 92 days it burned up in the earth's atmosphere. Four months after *Sputnik's* launch, the U.S. launched its first satellite, *Explorer 1*. It detected belts of radiation around the earth, later named the Van Allen belts.

SIMPLE SATELLITE
Launched by the Russian A1 rocket, *Sputnik 1* weighed 185 lb. It transmitted radio signals from its four antennae.

Orbiting Satellites

A satellite in a high-altitude, geosynchronous orbit—approximately 22,300 miles above Earth—circles our planet once every 24 hours, the same amount of time it takes the earth to spin on its axis. This means that it stays above the same part of Earth's surface all the time. At such a distance, the satellite can examine a vast portion of Earth's surface—this viewing area is called the satellite's footprint. Geosynchronous satellites are used to transmit thousands of global telephone calls and television signals every second.

Watching Earth

Many satellites are designed to watch Earth in some way. Since the launch of the first weather satellite, *Tiros 1*, in 1960, weather or meteorological satellites have helped monitor weather patterns and climate conditions as well as forecasting potentially dangerous weather systems, such as hurricanes. In the past, such disasters would strike with little warning. Satellites can also map the locations of minerals, water, and types of vegetation. As well as providing clues to where to find new resources, they help us understand how well, or poorly, people are managing Earth's ecology. For example, the satellite *Nimbus 7* discovered a hole in Earth's ozone layer.

> Science fiction writer Arthur C. Clarke predicted the development of satellites long before they were invented.

DIFFERENT ORBITS
Other orbits include the low-altitude orbit, the sun-synchronous (polar) orbit, and an elliptical Molniya orbit.

FACTS AND FIGURES

Between 900 and 1,000 new commercial satellites are due to be launched by the year 2008.

In 1984, *Solar Max*, launched in 1980, became the first satellite to be repaired in space by the space shuttle.

NASA estimates that there are 9,000 manmade objects orbiting Earth. Many of these are debris from rockets.

The largest satellite in orbit is the *Galaxy 11*. It weighs 4.5 tons and has a wingspan of 102 ft.

Intelsat's *Early Bird* satellite, launched in 1965, was the world's very first communications satellite.

WEATHER EYE
Weather satellites play a vital role in forecasting and following existing weather patterns. Hanging in geosynchronous orbits, such satellites monitor wind speed, clouds, sea temperature, and other conditions.

MAPPING
The *Landsat 4* satellite maps the earth. It can detect pollution or analyze rocks and minerals. It can even find oil.

SHUTTLE
Even the space shuttle carries remote sensing instruments for scanning and mapping Earth in detail.

EARLY SPACE MISSIONS

On April 12, 1961, in a mission lasting just one hour and 48 minutes, Russian cosmonaut Yuri Gagarin orbited Earth inside a tiny spacecraft, *Vostok 1*. His pioneering journey has led the way for hundreds of missions carrying people into space.

Fuel rockets jettisoned

Takeoff

CM reenters atmosphere

Splashdown

Pioneer Missions

The race into space saw both the Soviet Union and the United States accelerate their space programs. After the Soviets scored a collection of notable firsts, including the first man in space, the first woman in space, and the first space walk, attention shifted to getting a person onto the moon. Just seven years after Gagarin's historic journey, the U.S.'s *Apollo 8* became the first manned space vehicle to orbit the moon. Five months later, *Apollo 10* staged a dress rehearsal for a full-scale moon landing coming to within 9 miles of the moon's surface.

RUSSIANS IN SPACE
Yuri Gagarin's *Vostok 1* was the first of six Vostok crafts. Later Russian manned spacecrafts included Voskhod and Soyuz.

In 1975 a Soviet and an American craft docked in space. The crews shook hands to symbolize future cooperation.

FACTS AND FIGURES

The first living creature in space wasn't a human, but the dog Laika, launched in *Sputnik 2*.

By 2000, over 200 missions carried 400 people into space. Just 12 people have walked on the moon.

NASA stands for National Aeronautics and Space Administration. It is funded by the U.S. government.

The Apollo moon missions left more than 50 tons of discarded equipment on the moon's surface.

Early American manned space programs included the Gemini, Mercury, and Apollo crafts.

Vostok 3 and *4* were both launched on August 11, 1962. They orbited Earth in sight of each other.

Life On Board a Spacecraft

Conditions on board early spacecrafts were uncomfortable. Food was barely palatable, and crew members were forced to wear bulky space suits at all times because the cabins were unpressurized. Tragically, in 1971 the crew of the Soviet *Soyuz 11* died when their cabin depressurized. In space, all astronauts experience a lack of gravity known as weightlessness. This makes tasks such as eating, sleeping, and working much more difficult than on Earth. To cope with weightlessness, scientists developed basic showers, cooking equipment, and toilets on early missions. The facilities on board the space shuttle and space stations are far more sophisticated.

JUNK FOOD
The first space food was nutritious but unappetizing dried cubes and liquid mush. It has improved!

If not kept under control, liquid turns into a floating, spherical blob in weightless conditions.

CAREFUL
Weightlessness means that going to the bathroom in space is a tricky operation. Hand-holds and foot restraints keep the astronaut in place. A vacuum maintains a seal between the astronaut and the seat.

TO THE MOON (RED)
After the main fuel sections of the rocket are jettisoned, the command/service module (CSM) heads for the moon.

LM blasts off and rejoins CSM

Rocket heads to moon

CSM turns around and docks with lunar module (LM)

Command module (CM) detaches

Crew enter LM and land

HOME TO EARTH (PINK)
Part of the lunar module takes off from the moon and rejoins the command/service module before heading to Earth.

To the Moon

The most famous space mission to date is the first moon landing. On July 16, 1969, the massive Saturn V rocket launched the *Apollo 11* mission into space. In a complicated set of maneuvers, the command/service module (CSM), containing astronaut Michael Collins, orbited the moon while the lunar module, holding astronauts Neil Armstrong and Buzz Aldrin, descended to the moon's surface and landed late on July 20, 1969. Watched by over 600 million people on television, Armstrong and Aldrin stepped out onto the moon's surface the following morning, planted an American flag, and collected 48 pounds of rock and dust samples. Once back inside the lunar module, they blasted off and docked with the CSM, which then returned to Earth. The command module, with the astronauts on board, detached itself from the service module and splashed down in the Pacific Ocean on July 24, 1969. Six more Apollo missions followed.

MAKING HISTORY
Filmed by a camera mounted on the lunar module, *Eagle*, Neil Armstrong stepped tentatively out onto the moon's surface.

SPLIT PERSONALITY
The lunar module was a two-part craft. The crew blasted off from the moon in the top section, leaving the bottom half behind.

The longest time anyone has spent on the moon is 74 hours, 59 minutes, during the *Apollo 17* mission.

SPLASHDOWN
NASA's astronauts use parachutes to land their modules in the sea. Russia's cosmonauts usually come down on land.

DATABANK

Q Who was the first woman in space, and what nationality was she?

A Soviet Valentina Tereshkova orbited Earth in 1963. She was 26 years old.

Q Who performed the first walk in space and when did it happen?

A In 1965, Soviet cosmonaut Alexei Leonov made the first space walk.

SPACE SHUTTLE

Since the pioneering visits to the moon, the U.S. space program has been concentrated around the space shuttle. Versatile and reusable, the space shuttle has performed a variety of fascinating and daring tasks, from repairing broken satellites to ferrying astronauts to and from space stations.

FLIGHT DECK
The space shuttle pilot and the payload commander monitor a space walk from the flight deck.

Working Inside and Out

Astronauts' work on early missions was usually confined to reporting back to Earth on their own condition and that of their craft. Today they have a wider range of tasks to perform in missions that last up to a week. Many experiments—from growing crystals in space to testing new equipment—are undertaken inside the shuttle. Satellites and other space hardware are deployed from the shuttle's large cargo bay. This may involve the use of the remote manipulator system (RMS). This robot arm is controlled from inside the shuttle and can move huge amounts of cargo. Crew members wear EVA space suits (see page 55) in order to perform missions outside the craft.

CABIN
The shuttle and the robot arm are operated from the flight deck. Below this are the crew's quarters.

Capture and Repair

Some of the most vital work that space shuttle crews have engaged in has been correcting problems with probes, satellites, and telescopes already in space, but not working properly. A repair mission must first capture the object orbiting in space using a delicate set of maneuvers often involving the RMS robot arm and astronauts in EVA suits. Once the item is safely under control, it can be repaired before being released to perform its mission. In 1992, the STS-49 shuttle mission was extended by two days to capture the *Intelsat VI* satellite, which had been in an unusable orbit since its launch. Crew members fitted a live rocket motor to the satellite, which successfully propelled it into its correct orbit.

HUBBLE TROUBLE
Launched from the shuttle in 1990, the Hubble Space Telescope was repaired by a shuttle crew in 1993.

The capture and redeployment of the *Intelsat VI* satellite required a space walk of 8 hours, 29 minutes.

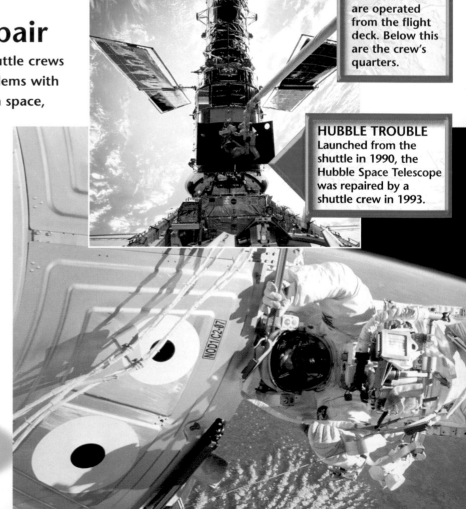

DATABANK

INPUT

Q Who is the oldest person to have traveled into space?

Q How many crew does a typical space shuttle mission carry?

Q What happened to the shuttle *Challenger*?

OUTPUT

A John Glenn, aged 77, aboard the space shuttle *Discovery*.

A Usually six or seven.

A It exploded after takeoff, killing its crew.

ROBOT ARM
Built by the Canadian Space Agency, the RMS robot arm weighs 1,348 lb, but can move cargo, such as satellites, weighing up to 66,169 lb. It has a maximum length of 50 ft., making it the longest robot arm in the world.

SPACELAB
The Spacelab module provided "shirtsleeve" conditions in which a host of experiments could be carried out.

Spacelab

Spacelab was a reusable space laboratory that operated within the cargo bay of a space shuttle. It was used on more than 25 space shuttle missions—almost a quarter of all shuttle flights—after its first launch in 1983. It was made up of a series of interchangeable modules. Some of these were pressurized and acted like an additional shuttle crew cabin, so that astronauts could work in regular clothing rather than pressurized space suits. In these modules, many microgravity experiments were carried out, observing the effect of extremely low gravity on a range of living things from eggs to plants and bacteria. Other Spacelab modules were unpressurized and known as external modules, or pallets. These contained instruments, such as telescopes and radiation monitors, that needed to be exposed to space. Different Spacelab missions used different combinations of modules.

> The X33-Venturestar may replace the shuttle. It will feature more reusable parts and make missions cheaper.

> Astronauts lose over 2 lb of weight for every six hours of space walking because it is such hard work.

HANGING OVER THE EARTH
Many shuttle missions are involved with building the *International Space Station*. This involves dozens of space walks.

FACTS AND FIGURES

The space shuttle orbiter is 120 ft. long, 57 ft. high, and has a wingspan of 79 ft. It weighs 187,360 lb.

The space shuttle weighs a fraction of a train engine, but delivers as much power as 39 locomotives.

Each of the space shuttle's solid rocket motors burns 5 tons of propellant per second.

Unlike early missions, the space shuttle offers a varied food menu that is only repeated every seven days.

Because of weightlessness, the crew exercises for two hours each day to keep their muscles and heart healthy.

Crew members must clean the shuttle every day to avoid a buildup of potentially dangerous dust.

LIVING IN SPACE

During the 1960s, manned missions into space were short.
The arrival of semipermanent space stations orbiting Earth
has enabled people to spend more time in space,
often conducting intriguing experiments.

GOING ON AND ON
Launched in 1986, the core module of *Mir*
weighed 21 tons. Later additions have
increased its weight to over 100 tons.

Salyut, Skylab, and *Mir*

The U.S.S.R.'s *Salyut* and U.S.'s *Skylab* space stations proved that people could stay in space for long
periods, even though weightlessness had some effects on blood circulation and muscle wasting.
Salyut and *Skylab* each had one docking port to receive
incoming space flights. The *Mir 1* space station, launched
in 1986, has six. These allow different craft and modules
to be joined with *Mir*, making it the largest structure in space.
Although plagued by problems, *Mir* is a success in many ways.
It set new records for long
stays in space and
paved the way for
the *International
Space Station (ISS)*.

There are plans to offer a short
stay on *Mir* as a grand prize on
a future TV game show.

SKYLAB
The U.S.'s first space
station, *Skylab*, was
launched in 1973 and
was built from parts
of a Saturn V rocket.

International Space Station (ISS)

The *ISS* is being pieced together by crews and flights
from the space shuttle and Russian rockets.
It will hold seven crew when
complete. Its massive arrays of solar
cells covering almost 4,856 square yards.
will generate 110kw of power. The *ISS* will perform
dozens of experiments in its six laboratories,
looking at the effects of microgravity on cells
and living organisms as well as developing
new materials and industrial
processes, which could
have great benefit
on Earth.

ISS OVERHEAD
The first section
of the *ISS* was
launched in
1998. It will
take between 44
and 46 missions
to complete the
290-ft.-long space
station. This
picture shows
what the finished
station may
look like.

The *ISS* space suit used for EVAs can be used 25 times before it must be returned to Earth for servicing.

Extravehicular Activity

Trips outside of the craft, either to deploy a satellite from a space shuttle's cargo bay or to work on a craft or space station, are called extravehicular activity or EVAs. For these, astronauts need a space suit (see below), which protects them from harmful radiation, extreme temperatures, and micrometeroids—fast-moving dust particles that could tear through regular clothing and flesh. The space shuttle's extravehicular mobility unit (EMU) is a suit made of many different layers of materials and is equipped with a main and reserve oxygen supply, 16 ounces of drinking water, and urine collection and climate control devices. The suit weighs over 106 pounds on Earth and takes 45 minutes to put on. Astronauts wearing the EMU suit can work outside in space for up to seven hours.

JET PACK
The manned maneuverd unit (MMU) is a backpack featuring jet thrusters that allow astronauts to move around in space.

In-suit drinking bag

Glove—tailored for each astronaut

Temperature control valve

Camera to relay pictures to the shuttle cockpit

Dark visor to reduce sun's glare

Space suit has many layers of materials

Computer display

Layers with cooling fluid to keep temperature constant

Boots—weighed down to counter weightlessness

DATABANK

Q Which was the world's first operational space station?

A The Soviet *Salyut 1* was launched in 1971. It was visited by one astronaut for 23 days.

Q How will garbage and waste that cannot be recycled be disposed of on the *ISS*?

A It will be returned to Earth or placed in a vehicle designed to burn up in the atmosphere.

FACTS AND FIGURES

The *International Space Station* is being built by 16 nations including the U.S., Russia, Japan, and the U.K.

Russian doctor Valeriy Poliyakov spent 437 days aboard *Mir* 1994–95—the longest ever space mission.

Crew members will perform around 850 hours of space walks during the *ISS's* assembly.

The *ISS* will have as much living and working space as the passenger compartments of two Boeing 747 jets.

Mir orbits 242 mi. above Earth. By August 2000 it had made 82,150 trips around Earth since it was launched.

Over three missions, Russian cosmonaut Sergei Avdeyev spent a total of 747.6 days in space.

In 1995 when the space shuttle *Atlantis* docked with *Mir,* they created the heaviest manmade object in space.

SPACE PROBES

Space probes are designed to leave Earth's orbit and head out into space to explore, measure, and send back information about other parts of the solar system and, potentially, the universe beyond.

FACTS AND FIGURES

The first probe to orbit another planet was *Mariner 9*, which flew around Mars in 1972.

In 1972, *Venera 8* landed on Venus. It was the first probe to successfully land on another planet.

Voyagers 1 and *2* each weigh over a ton, have 65,000 working parts, yet run on just 400w of power.

The *Helios B* probe came within 27 million mi. of the sun in 1976—the closest a probe has been.

The *Venera 13* and *14* probes were sent to Venus in 1982. They used drills to delve into the planet's crust.

The *Pioneer 10* probe is already 7 billion mi. from Earth and is heading toward the constellation of Taurus.

Better Than Humans

While humans are very adaptable, we cannot survive in space without tons of equipment. Probes are smaller and cheaper to build than crewed spacecraft because they do not need crew quarters, safety systems, and huge supplies of oxygen, water, and food. What is more, it is easier to protect mechanical and electrical parts than humans from the radioactivity, toxic chemicals, and extreme pressures and temperatures found on many of the solar system's planets. Most probes are launched with no hope of return—an unthinkable mission for people.

Probes to Mars have a high failure rate. At least a dozen Russian and U.S. missions have ended in disaster.

Orbiters and Flyby Probes

Probes are often classed according to whether they orbit, fly by, or land on a planet or satellite. Lander probes grab the headlines with their images of a planet surface beamed back to Earth, but probes like *Galileo,* which went into orbit around Jupiter in 1995, have revolutionized our knowledge of the planets and space. One of the oldest flyby missions is still considered the most spectacularly successful. Launched in 1977, *Voyager 1* is not only still working, but will continue to do so until its power fails in about 2020. *Voyager* completed its main mission with a final flyby of Neptune in 1989, but is now well into its second task, called the *Voyager* Interstellar Mission. This is designed to investigate features of the outer solar system, such as its magnetic field and solar wind.

Earth

Sun

Jupiter

BY JUPITER
Galileo needed a slingshot launch (see right) to reach Jupiter. It used the gravity of Venus and then Earth twice.

SLINGSHOT LAUNCH
A space probe's speed can be increased or its direction changed by using another planet's gravity as a free energy source.

On the Surface

Few landers have the ability to move from their position, but a small number of amazing robots have managed to trundle around a small part of the moon's, or another planet's, surface. The first of these were the *Lunokhod* robot rovers. These landed on the moon in 1970 and 1973 and were driven by remote control from Earth. In 1997, the *Pathfinder* probe opened its petallike panels and released the *Mars Sojourner* robot rover onto the surface of Mars. *Sojourner* was very successful in navigating its own way around the surface on its six wheels, analyzing rock and soil samples, and relaying the information back to *Pathfinder*, which then sent it back to Earth.

The *Pioneer Venus Orbiter* and *Multiprobe* were part of the same mission, but were launched separately in 1978.

MULTIPROBE
The *Venus Multiprobe* released one large and three smaller crafts to test the planet's surface and atmosphere.

LUNOKHOD
In preparation for putting a human on the moon, the Soviets sent two *Lunokhod* rovers to explore the lunar surface. These fragile vehicles sent back important data, but a Soviet crewed mission never took place.

The European Space Agency's Rosetta Mission will feature two probes. It will investigate a comet for two years.

DATABANK

Q What was the first space probe, and where did it go?

A The Soviet-built *Luna 2* successfully impacted with the moon's surface in 1959.

Q How many space probes are planned to be launched in the future?

A In the next 10 years 45 to 50 probes will visit planets, comets, asteroids, and deep space.

STAY OR GO?
The first probe to land on Mars was *Viking 1* in 1976. It could not move, but it sent back amazing pictures of the planet's surface (left). In 1997, the *Mars Sojourner* robot (above) could move around short distances. Its six wheels had studs for extra grip.

PIONEER VENUS LANDER
This large lander, 5 ft. wide, performed seven science experiments. It did not survive on Venus' harsh surface for long.

THE FUTURE IN SPACE

Since the first missions into space 40 years ago, we have built up an enormous knowledge of the universe. The future is likely to see many more exciting projects that will greatly increase our understanding.

 New Findings

By visiting places yet to be closely examined, future space probes and missions will help fill in some of the gaps in our knowledge of the solar system. For example, from around 2009 onward, the *Pluto-Kuiper Express* will examine Pluto and the far reaches of the solar system. Other probes will focus even farther afield. NASA's *Terrestrial Planet Finder (TPF)* will search for, map, and measure the characteristics of planets orbiting nearby star systems. It may even locate planets with conditions suitable for life.

It is difficult for people to travel out of the solar system because of the vast distances involved.

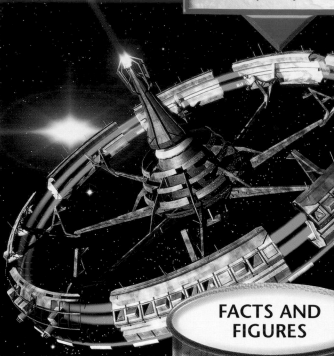

VACATION IN ORBIT
Plans are in place to build and launch space hotels for civilians. These would orbit Earth and could be in place by 2040.

 Are We Alone?

People are fascinated by the possibility of intelligent life existing elsewhere in the universe. The Search for Extraterrestrial Intelligence (SETI) organization monitors millions of radio signals we receive from the universe, searching for a pattern, which may indicate the presence of intelligent life. It is an enormous, ongoing task that may never reveal alien life. Yet many scientists find it hard to believe that throughout the entire universe, life only exists on our small planet, located on the outer edge of a modest-sized galaxy.

EARTH IS OURS
Many films have portrayed aliens as evil monsters in huge spaceships eager to take over Earth.

GREEN MEN
Aliens may come in any form. They could be made from different materials than animals on Earth.

FACTS AND FIGURES

NASA's *Terrestrial Planet Finder* will be launched in 2011, two years after its *Next Generation Space Telescope*.

The dangerous debris from space rockets that orbit Earth may be removed by a special laser, blasting device.

Future spacecraft may have sails to harness the power of the solar wind. This travels at up to 550 mi. per second.

Future Mars missions include *Mars Surveyor 2001 Orbiter* and Japan's *Nomozi*, which will arrive in 2003.

In 2003, NASA will send a pair of advanced rovers to Mars to search for signs of water. Each has 10 cameras.

To be launched in 2008, the *Laser Interferometer Space Antenna (LISA)* will hunt for black holes in distant galaxies.

New crystal materials for industry may be manufactured in the microgravity of space.

SPACE MINERS
As Earth's natural resources are used up, we may be forced to mine asteroids or try to beam down solar power from space.

People on Mars

Although researchers have not been able to confirm that any life exists on the red planet, this is unlikely to stop a future crewed mission there. The next wave of missions to Mars will include crewless probes that collect samples and return to Earth. These could be launched near the end of this decade. Before a crewed mission is attempted, crewless probes and robots would have to land in advance to set up some of the equipment vital to a Mars colony mission. These robots could build living quarters and even start to produce fuel.

NEW VENTURE
Astronauts on Mars will need lightweight space suits because the planet's gravity is greater than that of the moon. Energy is likely to be provided by solar panels, fuel cells, and maybe even nuclear reactions.

It would take today's spacecraft at least six months to a year to reach Mars.

Return to the Moon

It seems likely that a generation from now there will be a human presence on the moon. With no atmosphere and interference caused by millions of Earth radio signals, it would be the ideal place for an observatory with both radio and optical telescopes. It could also become a staging post for deep space missions with craft launched more efficiently from its low-gravity surface. Mineral deposits may attract lunar prospectors, while the thrill of entering space may see small numbers of moon tourists by 2040.

The moon's south pole is a likely site for a base because it receives constant sunlight, providing endless solar power.

Terraforming

Terraforming is the changing of another planet's environment to allow animals, plants, and humans to live there. Terraforming Mars would involve finding water, importing millions of microorganisms adapted for life on Mars, and generating vast amounts of atmospheric gases to trap heat and warm the planet's surface. The process would take many thousands of years, but may be attempted in the distant future.

MOVING ON FROM EARTH
Any settlements on the moon or other planets would have to be built from materials found on the planets themselves.

GLOSSARY

This section explains some of the more unusual or difficult terms that have been used in this book. The entries are arranged in alphabetical order.

ORBIT
The path of a satellite or moon around a planet. The time it takes to complete one orbit is called the orbital period.

Absolute magnitude The measure of the real brightness of an object. It measures a star's brightness as if viewed from 32.6 light-years away.

Acceleration The rate of change in the velocity of a moving object.

Active galaxy A galaxy with a large black hole at its center, which generates huge amounts of energy.

Apparent magnitude A measure of how bright a star appears to us on Earth.

Asteroid A rocky body in the solar system a few hundred miles (or less) in size.

Atmosphere The layer of gas surrounding a planet or moon.

Atom The smallest part of an element containing subatomic particles called electrons, protons, and neutrons.

Binary star Two stars in orbit around each other.

Black hole An object in space with such a strong gravitational pull that nothing can escape it.

Brown dwarf A failed star that did not get hot enough for core nuclear fusion to take place to create an actual star.

Cluster A group of stars or galaxies that affect each other by their gravitational attraction.

Comet An object made of dust and ice. When its orbit brings it close to the sun, some ice melts and creates a long tail in the sky.

Constellation A collection of stars grouped in an area of the night sky as viewed from Earth.

Dark matter Matter known to exist, but invisible—believed to make up much of the universe.

Electromagnetic waves Waves made of vibrations of constantly changing electrical and magnetic fields, such as light.

Electron A subatomic particle carrying a negative charge.

Escape velocity The speed at which an object must travel to escape another object's gravity.

Extraterrestrial Anything that originates or is located outside of Earth or its atmosphere.

BIG BANG
The theory that an immensely violent event billions of years ago gave birth to all the matter in the universe.

Galaxy A collection of millions or billions of stars, planets, gas, and dust bound together by gravity.

Gravity The force of attraction between objects.

Greenhouse effect The warming of a planet's atmosphere as heat from the sun is trapped by a layer of gas, such as carbon dioxide.

Infrared radiation A form of invisible electromagnetic radiation.

Light-year A measure of distance, it is how far light travels in one Earth year—5.88 trillion miles.

Luminosity A measure of how much light and heat a star gives out.

Magnetic field The area around a magnet in which magnetic force works. Planets can act as magnets.

Mass The amount of material in an object.

Meteorite A large meteor that impacts with Earth's surface.

Meteoroids Small rocky objects in space seen only when they burn up in Earth's atmosphere as meteors.

Neutrino A particle with no electrical charge or mass.

Neutron An uncharged subatomic particle.

Neutron star A collapsed star made up mainly of neutrons. Though small in size, neutron stars have an extremely high mass.

Nuclear fusion When two atomic nuclei produce a new nucleus. This releases a large amount of energy.

Nucleus (plural: nuclei) The protons and neutrons found at the core of an atom.

Oort Cloud A cloud of comets at the edge of the solar system.

Pressure The force exerted over an area by a gas, solid, or liquid.

Proton A subatomic particle that has a single positive charge.

Pulsar A spinning neutron star that sends radiation out into space.

Quasar A distant galaxy releasing enormous amounts of energy from a small central core.

Radiation Electromagnetic energy that travels in waves—given off by radioactive substances.

Red giant A bright red star, up to 100 times the size of the sun, believed to be at the end of its life.

Redshift An apparent increase in wavelength (becoming more red) of the light waves emitted from an object moving away from the observer.

Rotational period The time it takes a planet or star to rotate on its own axis.

Satellite An object that orbits another body. Includes artificial satellites.

Solar wind The stream of particles ejected from the sun into space.

Supernova The explosive death of a massive star once it has used up all its nuclear fuel.

Ultraviolet radiation A form of invisible electromagnetic radiation.

Velocity An object's speed, which is calculated by dividing the distance it has traveled by the time it took to travel the distance.

White dwarf A hot, very dense, compact star.

X rays A form of electromagnetic radiation that can pass through solid objects.

NEBULA (PLURAL: NEBULAE)
A large cloud of dust and gas found within a galaxy. New stars are formed inside nebulae

INDEX

ACKNOWLEDGMENTS

The publishers would like to thank the following:

 ## Photographs

p9(cr) NASA; p11(bl) NASA; p12(cl & tr) NASA; p14(cl) NASA; p15(bl) NASA; p19(cl) NASA; p20(cr) NASA; p21(bc) NASA; p22(tr & cr) NASA, (cl) Science Photo Library/John Sanford; p26(tl) NASA/Jeff Hester & Paul Scower (Arizona State University); p28(tr) NASA; p30-31(tl-br) Science Photo Library/David A Hardy; p31(tr) Science Photo Library/Chris Butler; p33(br) Science Photo Library; p34(cl) NASA; p35(bl) NASA/Robert Williams & the Hubble Deep Field Team (STScI); p37(bl) NASA; p39(tr) Mary Evans Picture Library; p44(bl) Science Photo Library/Francois Gohier; p45(tl) Science Photo LIbrary/Dr Fred Espenak, (c & bc & br) NASA; p49(bl & bcl & bc & bcr & br) NASA; p51(tr) NASA; p52(tl & c & br) NASA; p57(cl) NASA, (bl) NASA/Mary A Dale-Bannister, Washington University in St.Louis; p58(tr) Science Photo Library/Roger Harris; p60(tr) NASA; p61(bc) NASA/ESA/Andrew Fruchter/ERO Team (STScI)

 ## Artists & contributors

Every effort has been made to trace and credit the artists whose work appears in this book, and the publishers apologize to those whose names do not appear below:
John Marshall, Ray Grinway, Richard Ward , T. Hader, Nigel Quigley, John Ridyard, Ian Thompson, Gary Bines, Michael Roffe, Josephine Martino, Janos Marey, Lee Gibbons, M. Saunders, Chris Forsey, Robin Carter , Julian Baker, David Russell, Guy Smith, J. Matty, Jeremy Gower, Sebastian Quigley, R. Hayward, Terry Gabbey, Ron Jobson Marion Appleton, Jonathan Adams, Tom Connell and Michael E. Fisher

Design
Mik Gates